THE L FACTOR

DR IAN JAGELMAN

IDENTIFYING AND DEVELOPING CHRISTIAN LEADERS

Ark House Press
PO Box 1722, Port Orchard, WA 98366 USA
PO Box 1321, Mona Vale NSW 1660 Australia
PO Box 318 334, West Harbour, Auckland 0661 New Zealand
arkhousepress.com

This book is a new edition—with a new title, new format and new design, but with the same contents—of Identifying and Developing Christian Leaders (published by Openbook Publishers in 2002).

First Edition:
First printing October 2005 Second printing December 2010 Third printing September 2011
Second Edition: First printing August 2013

National Library of Australia Cataloguing-in-Publication entry
Jagelman, Ian, 1945–
The L factor : identifying and developing Christian leaders. ISBN 1 921144 01 7.
Leadership. 2. Christian leadership. I. Title. 253
Published by: The Jagelman Institute
PO Box 337, Parramatta New South Wales 2124
admin@jaginst.org, www.jaginst.org

Printed and distributed by Ingram
Design and layout by initiateagency.com

To Richard Botta, Richard Green, Kenn Iskov
and the other wonderful leaders who have worked with me in
serving the Christian City Congregations at Lane Cove, Carlingford
and Ryde in Sydney, Australia

PREFACE

Four years ago I took to Russia the drafts of two chapters from my book, *The Empowered Church, Releasing Ministry through Effective Leadership* (Open Book Publishers, 1998), to teach to a group of Russian pastors. I am back in Russia with the Russian translation now in my possession ready to put pen to paper again.

In the three years since its first edition I have taught its content in various countries to many hundreds of pastors and leaders. They have found its central concept, 'The distinction between leadership and ministry', a catalyst for re-evaluating their personal priorities and the basis for re-examining the structures of the churches or organisations they serve.

Some denominational structures are more difficult to change or adapt than others. However, many of those who have read the book, or attended a seminar, have said it gave practical insight into both a need for change and how it might be achieved.

The book was about a concept — the confusion which exists between leadership and ministry. During the seminars people frequently asked me questions about leaders. Typical of these questions are the following three:

- 'Are leaders born or made?'
- 'How can you identify someone as a potential leader?'
- 'What can we do to develop leaders?'

It is my aim in this book to attempt to answer these questions.

In *The Empowered Church* Psalm 78:72 is introduced as pivotal to my basic paradigm and Philippians 2:22 had a similar impact on me as I prepared to write this book. I would like to encourage you to pause now and meditate on this verse:

But you **know** that Timothy "has **proved** himself": because "**as a son**" with his father" – he has served with me "**in the work** of the gospel". (NIV) (*structure mine*)

God has called many of us to be fathers or mothers to develop sons and daughters for the work of the gospel.

Ian Jagelman *Socci, Russia October, 2001*

CONTENTS

CHAPTER ONE

THE LEADERSHIP DEVELOPMENT PARADIGM - AN OVERVIEW

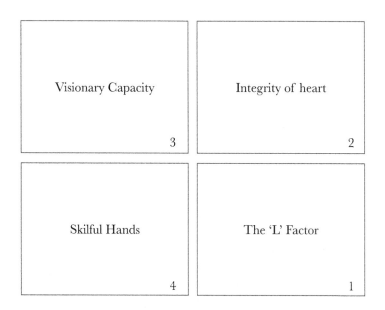

Visionary Capacity ... 3	Integrity of heart ... 2
Skilful Hands ... 4	The 'L' Factor ... 1

Quadrant One

In early 1999 a new Christian Institute[1] attached to Macquarie University in Sydney decided to explore what they might offer in the way of post-graduate training for Christian leaders. They invited a small group of people involved in education, management consulting and institutional leadership to meet. I was invited as someone who had successfully built a large organisation from the ground up. We were

1 The Macquarie Christian Studies Institute

asked to consider what a course might look like which integrated leadership theory (as taught in graduate MBA programmes), Christian ethics, biblical principles and the context of Christian ministry.

In preparing to chair the team's discussion (I had little hope of 'leading' them), I constructed the quadrant at the beginning of this chapter.

Quadrants two, three and four were relatively clear in most of our minds and shall be discussed throughout this book. However, quadrant one, what I now refer to as the 'L' factor, intrigued me. It is discussed in Chapter 2.

Quadrant Two

The second quadrant of the paradigm identifies 'integrity of heart' (Ps 78:72) as an essential prerequisite for the Christian leader. In *The Empowered Church* I observed that historical writing on Christian leaders and leadership had largely focussed on issues of character and spirituality. I do not wish to minimise the importance of this facet of the development of leaders. However, in truth, I feel I have little to add to what has already been written.

In the conclusion (pg 95) I briefly explore the implications of Philippians 2:22 as a mentoring process for leadership formation and at that time the 'servant' aspect of discipleship will raise issues related to the heart of a leader.

Another quality I shall touch on is the issue of generosity of spirit!

Quadrant Three

The third quadrant recognises that leaders of 21st-century churches and organisations lead in a context in which the speed of change requires as much flexibility as foresight. Although large corporations continue to undertake what are called 'business plans' the process has become more important than the plan which it produces. As leaders they engage in strategic conversations about the future. This requires skills I believe can and need to be taught. Chapter 8 gives tools to be used in such conversations.

Leaders need to be able to recognise 'the signs of the times' and be ready to reposition the resources and programming of the church to adapt to rapid social change. Such leaders need to be identified early and be given exposure to highly effective models in terms of both other leaders and innovative tools.

A friend and mentor (Tony Golsby-Smith) introduced me to Aristotle's

Rhetoric. Unless you are a glutton for punishment I wouldn't recommend you try to read the essay. However, within the essay is an insight often overlooked and yet critical to our own age.

Aristotle recognises that we often struggle to answer questions for which there is no right answer, but only a good answer. If there is a right answer then information, logic and time is all that is required. Put simply one plus one, even in a post-modern world, is rightly two.

If, however, it is not possible to have adequate information (ie, due to chaos or change), then logic does not provide the means for developing a right answer. In such circumstances intuition either augments or replaces reason as the primary tool of the leader. In some church traditions this intuitive process may be called 'revelation'. However, the notion of 'revelation' may be intimidating to some and objectionable to others. As a leader I cannot *depend* on revelation but am greatly helped on those few occasions when it occurs.

Some may have instances of revelation but all have the capacity for intuition. Many have lost the ability to use it due largely to our education systems. As leaders most of us need to be taught how to get in touch with our intuition as a tool in the planning process. Exercises such as 'mind mapping' are a beginning point for those who struggle with problems requiring intuitive processes. Mind mapping is touched on in Chapter 8 and I have included in *Suggested Reading* (pg 98) some further reading relating to this area. A leadership development paradigm would do well to include an exploration of the intuitive side of our thinking processes.

Quadrant three also includes the purpose versus vision debate. I am told that some leaders of religious orders say 'you can determine the future by looking at the past'. In doing budget forecasts this is frequently the case. A study of salvation history often reveals not just God's overall plan (*oikonomia*) but also the plot (hypothesis).

Many Christian leaders derive from Scripture a biblical purpose for their church or organisation which then governs their choice of programmes and priorities. Saddleback Community Church in California is an outstanding example of this. Chapter 2 of *The Empowered Church* gives guidance on how to implement this kind of purpose-driven approach.

Other leaders are vision driven. In biblical terms these are the seers. When they are 'in the Spirit' they have revelations of land and buildings and nations and multitudes coming to Christ. They inspire commitment through language such as 'God has shown me' rather than 'the Bible says'. They allow the Scriptures to totally govern their beliefs in terms of doctrine and morality but lead, in terms of future directions, by way of vision. It is how the gift of faith operates in their ministries.

In the book, *Church Growth: State of the Art*[2], Elmer Towns describes the three ways the gift of faith may work in highly effective leaders. He also describes the way dominant but not exclusive patterns of behaviour may be identified.

1   Faith in the **instruments** given by God to the church. Different leaders focus on different instruments (eg, Bible teaching, the sacraments, signs and wonders and others).

2   Faith in **insight** from God. These are the mystics among us who can emerge from a prayer time with God with a dream or vision which inspires their church to fulfil a biblical mandate. Like the prophets of old they face the risk of being totally right or totally wrong. They are not common in any religious tradition (including Pentecostalism) but nor are they absent from any (including Evangelicalism). Leaders like Hudson Taylor come into this category.

2 Wagner, C Peter. *Church Growth: State of the Art*. Tyndale House Publishers, 1986.

3   Faith in the **intervention** of God. These are the prayer warriors like George Muller who made the ministry of Hudson Taylor possible.

A leadership development paradigm needs to affirm the validity of each expression of the gift of faith and help leaders discover how the gift of faith operates in their lives and ministries. What it ought not do is elevate one expression above the other two and so undermine a potential leader's belief in their capacity to lead.

Also I think it is wrong to assume that visionary leaders, who lead in faith derived from insights from God, are necessarily always mystical. This comes back to the fact that when God made us he gave us brains capable of both cognitive and intuitive processes. The danger is one of labels. Some leaders who call themselves prophetic may merely be very intuitive. And others who call themselves intuitive may be prophetic.

Some purpose-driven leaders are also very intuitive and powerfully prophetic.

In identifying and developing leaders labels can be very destructive, particularly with young emerging leaders.

It is my conviction that some people are born with capacities which enable an astute recruiter to identify them as potentially highly performing leaders. In the chapters which follow, two such capacities are discussed in detail (intellectual strength which gives a capacity for good judgment, and intellectual dexterity which gives a capacity for coping with complexity).

To those involved in recruiting future leaders I shall identify the things to look for as early indicators of potential. I shall introduce you to the thinking of researchers who have been exploring this general subject for many years.

Both the United Kingdom and United States military establishments believe future generals can be identified when they undertake their first officer training course! However identification of potential (the nature factor) does not negate the need for intentional training (the nurture factor). To my limited knowledge neither the UK nor the US have ever made a recruit a general after his or her first course.

Later in this book I shall introduce you to five levels of leadership. Each level requires an increasing capacity for judgment and dealing with complexity. I will offer a pathway for leadership development which recognises these levels and discusses the leadership styles appropriate as people are moving from level to level. I shall include an outline of job descriptions for each level and the qualifications required to move from one level to another. I shall raise the possibility of linking salary scales to where staff fit in terms of these levels.

In the book, *Built to Last*[3], the authors identify leaders as "clock makers not time tellers". Whilst a child can be taught to tell the time, making a clock is the task of a skilled craftsperson. The tasks of identifying and developing leaders ought not be seen as beyond our reach — a mystery known only to the members of a secret guild.

Our churches need competent leaders functioning at many levels. Leaders who have been identified early, have received appropriate training, and who have been placed in contexts where they can fully develop their potential. They need coaching and mentoring. They need discipling and disciplining.

They will benefit greatly if they can be part of a leadership development paradigm.[4]

Quadrant Four

Quadrant four relates to the many skills which leaders need and can acquire from effective training. *The Empowered Church* is being used extensively for this purpose. Since this book is about 'leaders' rather than 'leadership' I have limited any material on skills to Chapter 8 so quadrant four is identified in the model but not discussed in any depth.

---

3 Collins, James C. and Porras, Jerry I. Built to Last. Harper Business, 1997.
4 The outcome of the MCSI meetings was that two of the participants, Dr Robert Banks and myself, developed a 10 day program jointly run by MCSI and the Australian College of Ministry — in conjunction with the Fuller Seminary Doctor of Ministry program.

PART A

IDENTIFYING LEADERS

CHAPTER TWO

THE L FACTOR

Greensville Baptist Church had been growing steadily requiring continual changes to its programme and pastoral staff. After many years of vital growth in its two morning services, at long last the evening service was established and it was time to appoint someone to lead this potentially vital ministry. Senior Pastor Stephen Campbell was interviewing a prime candidate for the position. Roger was an architect by profession and had been active in lay ministry prior to being called into pastoral ministry. After getting good grades in his theology degree he had been asked to go to a new housing area to pioneer a church plant. It had grown well to about 100 then plateaued. Roger then decided it was time for further study and he resigned to undertake a post-graduate degree. After a number of years of active ministry he and his wife were applying to join Greensville as part of the pastoral team. What Pastor Stephen needed to know was whether Roger would make a good leader. We pick up the interview after pleasantries have been completed and they are getting down to business.

Ps Stephen: Roger, why do you think you were successful as a church planter?

Roger: Honestly, I think I was simply the right person in   the right place, at the right time. There was a small group of enthusiastic Christians who had moved into the area with their families looking for a church. It was really one big happy family. I took the Sunday service and preached regularly. When pastoral issues cropped up I tended to handle them without too much fuss. There was such a strong sense of community, everyone got involved without much direction and people were saved because the people were so infectious. I wasn't really the leader. I was more like one of them with a special gift because of my training.

Ps Stephen: Why did you leave?

Roger: Sometimes I wish I hadn't! But they didn't seem to need me and I have always had a strong desire to read and learn and thought I would grab the chance to do more study while our kids were still young.

Ps Stephen: When you finished your studies you sought an academic rather than a pastoral role. Why was that?

Roger: With three university degrees it just seemed the next logical step. I guess after prayer we though that the Lord was providentially leading us that way.

Ps Stephen: The position we are seeking to fill is predominantly a leadership role. What do you think you would bring to the position that others might not?

Roger: I have a great love of people and am strong pastorally. But I am also a keen student of contemporary culture. I believe that in my preaching I can relate well to young people. Young people need their questions answered and I believe I can do this.

Pastor Stephen pondered over what he was hearing most of which he had heard before in casual snippets over coffee at church events. He really liked Roger and respected his integrity and spirituality and yet…
Roger got the job but only lasted a few years. Something was missing! It is what I have come to call the 'L' factor.

The Big Picture

The next three chapters will discuss in depth the three elements of the 'L' factor which I have already identified as:
* a developed **belief system**;

- a capacity for **sound judgment**; and
- a capacity to **handle complexity**.

But in this short transition chapter I want to discuss the impact of the synergy of these three qualities.

Roger didn't struggle because he lacked gifts. He didn't struggle because he didn't relate well to people. He didn't struggle because he didn't work hard or maintain his personal spiritual disciplines. He struggled to succeed because leadership did not come easily to him.

Many people have offered definitions of leadership. Some are highly complex and others very simple. There is also the important distinction between direct leaders (who lead organisations or institutions) and indirect leaders (who lead through their ideas). My definition of leadership is 'any activity which directs, influences, or facilitates ministry by others'.[5]

Roger had the capacity to be an indirect leader but direct leadership extends beyond writing, teaching and preaching. It involves an individual influencing the destiny of an organisation and its members through decisions made. Decisions reflect a strongly-held belief system. Decisions must be clear and timely and deal with the future and not just the present. Decisions frequently are made in the midst of complex circumstances and multiple options. A 'direct leader' enjoys the decision making process and is frustrated with lack of decisiveness and uncertainty.

The highly effective leader seems to thrive on the opportunity to give direction and also sees ministry as important in terms of his or her calling. Leadership comes from within whereas ministry is activity in response to external need. The following diagram is based on the passage Mark 1:32–39 which reads as follows:

That evening after sunset the people brought to Jesus all the sick and demon-possessed. [33] The whole town gathered at the door, [34] and Jesus healed many who had various diseases. He also drove out many demons, but he would not let the demons speak because they knew who he was. [35] Very early in the morning, while it was

5 Jagelman, I. *The Empowered Church.* Openbook Publishers, 1998, p 9.

still dark, Jesus got up, left the house and went off to a solitary place, where he prayed. [36] Simon and his companions went to look for him, [37] and when they found him, they exclaimed: "Everyone is looking for you!" [38] Jesus replied, "Let us go somewhere else — to the nearby villages — so I can preach there also. That is why I have come". [39] So he traveled throughout Galilee, preaching in their synagogues and driving out demons.

Diagram 2.1: Leadership versus Ministry

In *The Empowered Church*, the focus was so much on leadership that some pastors who read it felt I was saying that leadership was more important than ministry. That was never my intention but I retain my conviction that 'ministry builds people but leadership builds churches', and that if we do not have healthy growing churches then

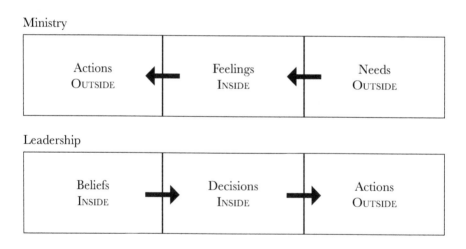

our capacity to minister is severely restricted.

In the passage above we can clearly see the tension between ministry and leadership in the life and mission of Jesus. In verses 32–34 the top half of the above diagram is depicted. In the evening those with needs are brought to the house where Jesus is staying. He sees the need, has feelings of compassion for them which move him to minister healing and deliverance to them.

However, the next morning (verses 36–39) the bottom half of the diagram is depicted. Jesus leaves his disciples to be alone so that he might pray. While he is away the needy crowds return and his disciples seek him that he might minister to them. But Jesus now assumes the role of leader. Without losing his compassion he is aware that God has a purpose for him to fulfil. Inspired by his beliefs rather than by the obvious needs, he decides they must move on to other villages where he can preach, because, as he states, "For this purpose I have come" (cf John 18:37).

It takes a 'strong belief'[6] system to overcome the power of needs when the capacity to meet them is apparently present. We can see this at work frequently in the mission of Jesus. He will choose to heal a single individual when others who are equally needy are present (John 5:1–10). We see not just the presence of a belief system but decision making based on it. Equally we can see strategic decisions being made in a complex situation. He acts so that what he believes about the plans and purposes of God might be fulfilled!

From that time on Jesus began to explain to his disciples that he must go to Jerusalem and suffer many things at the hands of the elders, chief priests and teachers of the law, and that he must be killed and on the third day be raised to life.

Peter took him aside and began to rebuke him. "Never, Lord!" he said. "This shall never happen to you!" Jesus turned and said to Peter, "Get behind me, Satan! You are a stumbling block to me; you do not have in mind the things of God, but the things of men". (Matt 16:21–23)

The same can be said about the life and mission of Paul (see Gal

---

6 I have wrestled with the term or phrase to use to describe the inner convictions or beliefs which drive leaders. The terms 'purpose' or 'calling' were considered but seem to me to reflect a single focus. Whereas 'belief systems' captures the multitude of convictions most leaders have as to not just what they should do but also how they should do it! 'Beliefs', rather than 'belief system', was also considered but it does not reflect the integrated nature of the convictions of leaders.

2:7–10; Eph 3:2–8, Col 1:24–29).

In Matthew 10:1–42 we see the interaction between Jesus the leader (decisions based on beliefs) and the ministry of the 12 he is sending out. Their ministry is to be governed by his beliefs.

In Roger's case he had beliefs but a combination of the complexity of the evening service, and a fear of making bad decisions made him hesitant and unable to give focus and direction to others in his ministry team.

Stephen thought back over the initial interview. The clues were there but at the time he was still learning how to identify a person's capacity for sound judgment (intellectual firepower) and dealing with complexity. Roger also learned that he would fit best in a situation where his ministry gifts worked with the leadership ability of another.

The implications of the distinction between ministry and leadership

In this second edition of "The L Factor" I wish to include some new material which has emerged through teaching, mentoring and consulting organisations embracing the ministry/leadership distinction.

I have intentionally kept it short in the hope it will provoke further discussion and research.

The focus of ministry and leadership is different:

Ministry	Leadership
Experience	Building
Events	Processes
People	Structures
Feelings	Goals
Needs	Beliefs
Caring	Gathering
Success	Effectiveness
Present	Future

What needs to be looked for in the profile of a leader is not always the same as what needs to be found in a minister:

Profile of:

Minister	Leader
Character	Character
Gift	Aptitude
Compassion	Beliefs
Faithfulness	Vision
Responsibility	Gatherers
Listeners	Builders

The training of ministers and leaders is also different:

Ministry	Leadership
Gift Discovering	Capacity Discovery
Gift Development	Skill Development
Gift Deployment	Belief Development

CHAPTER THREE

INTELLECTUAL STRENGTH

Pastor Bob needed a new youth leader for the junior youth ministry of the church. He had reduced the potential appointees down to two (Kevin and Sue) and was struggling to differentiate between them. He suspected either one could fulfil the role but the ministry had struggled for years and he was looking for someone special.

They seemed to have similar training and experience and were equally committed to the core values of the church. They both seemed enthusiastic about the position and even after prayer he was not sure what to do. He rang his friend Ivan who seemed to have a knack for choosing the right people for leadership positions.

To his great surprise Ivan suggested he invite Kevin and Sue to dinner at a Chinese restaurant and indicated he would be happy to attend. Two weeks later the dinner took place, and as far as Bob could tell nothing much of significance occurred or was discussed. On the way home in the car Ivan shocked Bob with the statement "Sue is definitely better suited to leadership". Quickly Bob thought back over the evening but still couldn't figure out what had caused his friend to be so definite about the choice. Finally he gave in and asked his friend the obvious question "Why?"

With a twinkle in his eye Ivan simply said "Kevin took too long to choose from the menu, he obviously struggles with decision making and will make a less effective leader".

Surely leadership doesn't come down to choosing between rice and noodles?! And yet time proved that the decision to appoint Sue was a good one.

Intellectual strength is not to be compared with IQ. For reasons which I shall explain IQ is often a poor indicator of who might become a highly effective leader.

At this point I want to introduce you to the research and writings of Howard Gardner from the Harvard Graduate School of Education. Gardner, an educationalist, has spent years studying the early detection and development of highly gifted children.

Gardner defines 'intelligence' as "The ability to solve a problem or fashion a product that is valued in at least one culture or community".[7] In his book, *Frames of Mind*,[8] he identifies seven different 'intelligences' which are as follows:

1   Linguistic (the ability to manipulate language effectively, the archetype being the poet).
2   Logical mathematical (the ability to manipulate symbols, typical of the successful scientist).
3   Spatial (the ability to process information continuously in three dimensions, like a sailor or sculptor).
4   Musical (the ability to manipulate sound in a complex way, like a composer or, combined with the following, a performer).
5   Bodily kinaesthetic (the ability for bodily coordination as found in the highest level of athletes and dancers).
6   Interpersonal (the ability to know what is happening between people and to mobilise it, as do good teachers and salespeople).
7   Intrapersonal (the ability for self-understanding without which all the others may be distorted in use).

Gardner assumes most great leaders will possess five of the seven intelligences. He also believes they emerge rather than are discovered.

Alistair Mant, in *Intelligent Leadership*[9] puts this theory to the test by examining the lives of some Australians who have risen to prominence as leaders. None of those chosen were Christian leaders nor

7 Gardner, H. *Frames of Mind: The Theory of Multiple Intelligences*. Basic Books, 1993
8 Gardner, H. *Frames of Mind: The Theory of Multiple Intelligences*. Basic Books, 1993, p 73–276
9 Mant, A. *Intelligent Leadership*. Allen & Unwin, 1997.

were any in an overtly religious context. Consequently I have undertaken my own examination of a few prominent Christian leaders whose gifts I have been able to uncover.

Remember, however, here we are dealing with outstanding leaders. One such example is Pastor Phil Pringle, founder of the Christian City Church movement.

Pastor Pringle, who has built one of Australia's largest churches, is someone I have known for many years and is someone who I could observe with little difficulty.

Phil is a poet, artist, songwriter, musician, athlete and has excellent interpersonal and intrapersonal skills!

The thing which surprised me was I had never linked these 'intelligences' which Phil possesses to his leadership ability.

What I want to explore with you is an understanding of the nature of the relationship which exists between these 'intelligences' and leaders. Each represents a form of dexterity. A form of intellectual agility.

In each of the intelligences there is a capacity to hold and wrestle with images (words, symbols, numbers, sounds etc.) and manipulate them so they take shape, form a sequence, establish a pattern or rhythm or give meaning to what others might assume to merely be random or chaotic events.

They can see either order or the potential for order. They can hear progression or the potential for progression. They sense potential within themselves and others and how that potential might be activated.

In other words they hear the next note before it is played, they see the next word before it is written. They can sense where the wind will come from and be ready to trim the sails.

They have the advantage of possessing the capacities that make decision making possible even under duress. In fact they have often anticipated and processed an issue well before it arises and are ready with their considered opinions when others are thinking about it for the first time.

For this reason they do not function well in organisations which have committees rather than teams. They enjoy brainstorming but have little tolerance of those they perceive to be intellectually slow. This is not necessarily an arrogance but more an impatience because their minds have already turned to other things.

It is important to put all this into perspective. Even a nation has few great leaders. Churches produce them occasionally and books are written about them. If they are indirect leaders (ie, those who exert influence but hold no leadership position within an organisation) their writing endures from generation to generation (eg, Jonathan Edwards and John Calvin).[10] This chapter is not about potentially great leaders, it is about identifying people with leadership potential. What 'multiple intelligences' research offers us is the awareness that judgment may be the fruit of abilities not an ability itself.

If I am considering someone for a leadership position I look for the presence of mental dexterity. I ask questions and listen to conversations.

I was listening recently to a series of sermons by Bill Hybels. I know he is an outstanding leader — his church is clear evidence of that. But what a wonderful storyteller he is! I gather he is an above average sailor. I wonder if he is musical?

It is difficult to describe how mental agility (as reflected in multiple intelligences) is linked to judgment. It is easier to see its link to dealing with complexity. Therefore judgment is more the capacity to 'respond' to complexity whereas intelligence is the capacity to grasp the issues. Former US President Jimmy Carter (a highly intelligent man) was criticised for his incapacity to make decisions, not for his lack of intelligence.

So both 'judgment' and 'multi-intelligences' will be present in highly effective leaders.

Oh by the way, I forgot to tell you that Sue who got the job is in the women's state fencing team and plays flute in an ensemble!!

---

10 See the discussion about the distinction between direct and indirect leaders on page 21.

CHAPTER FOUR

IDENTIFYING AND MODIFYING BELIEFS

Diagram 4.1: Levels of belief

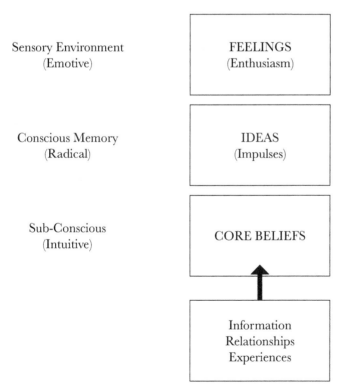

Sensory Environment
(Emotive)

FEELINGS
(Enthusiasm)

Conscious Memory
(Radical)

IDEAS
(Impulses)

Sub-Conscious
(Intuitive)

CORE BELIEFS

Information
Relationships
Experiences

Bill and John were pastors of large churches in the same denomination. Both were widely respected and influential in the direction of their movement. They were comfortable socially and frequently preached in one another's church. They had known each other for many years and there had only been one brief period of time when their relationship almost came apart.

For a few years they had both served on the denomination's executive council and on one occasion Harry, the council chairman, had to step in before there was a fist-fight. It almost seemed like there were two bulls in the same paddock and only one cow. To mix my metaphors they were both, in the opinion of others, pig headed.

Strongly Held Beliefs

This is the second facet of the 'L' factor. There are many definitions of leadership, the most simple being that leadership is 'influence'. It is my conviction that Jesus led his disciples by influencing them (through word and deed) to change their beliefs to become consistent with his own (see Matt 16:21–23).

The presence of an established belief system is a requirement for an effective leader. In developing leaders one has to both impart beliefs and modify faulty beliefs. This chapter explores how this may be done by:
- describing different levels of belief;
- discussing where beliefs come from; and
- suggesting how beliefs can be modified.

At this point it is important to state that I am neither a psychologist nor a psychiatrist. The model I present is the product of my own reflection and is not backed by the kind of research and scholarship behind the previous chapter.

I present it as a model which is sound enough to validate my overall point, rather than seeking to compete with psychological models which are the fruit of years of hard work.

The issue I want you to consider is that **effective leaders are**

able to lead because they know what they believe. This seems to be more important than what they actually believe. For example two effective leaders in the same city may come from very different theological positions. One may be Baptist and the other Pentecostal. Over time they may modify what they believe. But if they aren't confident as to what they believe (now) they would not be able to effectively lead.

Christians often confuse what they feel, what they think and what they really believe. In the early church there was a difference between what was believed (by the people), what was preached (by the clergy) and what was confessed (by the church).[11]

In this chapter I want to explore the process by which belief systems develop and then suggest a strategy by which they may be modified.

> Levels of Belief

Diagram 4.1 at the beginning of this chapter portrays three levels of belief. Although they are described as feelings, ideas and core beliefs, suggesting that only the third level are real beliefs, leaders often express their feelings and ideas as beliefs. Each of these three levels seems to penetrate more deeply into our conscious and subconscious minds. And so I want to discuss how these levels of belief occur before suggesting ways in which they may be modified.

>> Feelings

What we feel is an emotive response to a sensory environment influenced by previous experience. In other words the way we feel is influenced both by what is happening to us externally, and our recollection of past experience. We are all aware that two people in the same environment may react very differently or in the same way at different levels of intensity. For example two leaders attending a Christian conference may respond very differently to a strong appeal by the conference leader for a commitment to world missions. One

---

11 Pelikan, J. *The Emergence of the Catholic Tradition (100-600)*. University of Chicago, 1971.

may respond with great enthusiasm and mentally begin to pack for the next mission's trip. The other may respond with indifference, although at a conference 10 years before he or she had responded with the same level of enthusiasm as the other leader.

Why the difference? One of the leaders was hearing the appeal for the first time and responding with a level of idealism. The other was responding in the light of the negative experience which occurred following the conference 10 years before.

If asked, both leaders would probably defend their feelings as being an expression of their beliefs. And at one level the statement is true. However, it is also true to say that our feelings are fickle and as belief indicators they are not reliable. They are at best a temporary indication of what we believe as indicated by the following two examples.

Susan, the children's pastor, storms into the senior pastor's office at one o'clock on Sunday afternoon fuming about the lack of cleanliness in the toilets. As she bursts into the office, without knocking, she says, "If the toilets aren't clean next Sunday I'm quitting. It's my reputation at stake". Her expression is full of passion and she has no doubts in the world that she believes absolutely what she currently feels. A few hours later when she is sitting at home with her husband having a cup of coffee after lunch, a smile comes to her face which causes her husband to ask what she is smiling about. She responds by saying to her husband that he should have seen the pastor's face as she stormed in and out. In fact, she loves her role as the pastor to the children of the church, has no intention whatever of resigning next week, but the threat felt like a good thing to say at the time. She also felt quite secure that Pastor Richard, who had worked with her for many years, would know that these strongly expressed feelings were not a true indication of her core beliefs. The issue she was so upset about was important for the children and would, she hoped, be addressed in the near future.

Her husband also now had a smile on his face. He realised that often his wife expressed her feelings strongly in the same way he expressed his ideas.

David Brayshaw had grown up in a Roman Catholic family and had attended church until his early teens at which time he had rebelled. University had confirmed his suspicions about the church of his family and he considered himself an agnostic rather than an atheist. Since beginning work he had become attracted to another member of staff who was a member of the Pentecostal church. He decided to go along to a service with her.

There were many things about the service which were alien to him. It was not held in a traditional church building, there were no stained glass windows, no organ, no pews, no pulpit and no priest dressed in clerical garb. The service was being held in a school building, there was a band on the stage. The preacher spoke from a lectern and was dressed in casual clothes.

From the recesses of his religious upbringing there was a belief system telling him that this was not really a church. And yet his feelings were responding positively to the casual environment, the contemporary worship and the relevance of what the preacher was saying.

Although a person with highly developed cognitive faculties it surprised him that he was assessing the situation based on his feelings rather than on what he thought. And then it occurred to him that his previous rejection of the church of his family was not based on intellectual processes but rather on what he felt at the time. He knew he didn't want a belief system based on feelings, but he recognised the power of a positive environment which caused one to question previously held beliefs.

Ideas

I do not consider myself to be computer literate. I have a computer in my office and another one at home. Due to the technical assistance provided by the administrator at church, and my sons at home, I have had a number of computer programs installed. By and large these programs are user friendly and I have learnt to distinguish between an icon on a computer and an icon in a church.

It is fair to say my understanding is superficial. However, one term I have grasped, I think is RAM. I have been informed that this is a kind of memory that a computer has, which is temporary. The information within this memory is accessible on the screen of the computer, but the moment the computer is turned off the memory disappears. In other words it is randomly accessible but once the computer is switched off it is lost. I have also been told that there is other information stored on the hard drive of the computer (but don't ask me how) which is not lost when the computer is turned off. And so can be re-accessed at will.

I consider RAM a good analogy of the nature of a belief system expressed in the ideas a person holds at any one point in time. They are held in the conscious memory of the person, and are rational in nature, but are soon forgotten. Again let me use narrative to describe the nature of this level of belief.

Gary attends a weekly Bible study at the place where he works. The members of the Bible study group attend a variety of churches from different denominational backgrounds. At one such gathering Gary hears a Bible study presented by a fellow worker who attends the Seventh Day Adventist church. The Bible study presents the merits of a vegetarian diet and the case is made based on various verses from the Scriptures. Gary, who is overweight, is attracted to this idea as a way of losing weight and goes home to his wife to announce he has become a vegetarian. His 16 year old daughter, Kathleen (along with a number of girlfriends, who have been vegetarians for six months), is enthusiastic about her dad's idea. For the next five days Gary eats only vegetarian food until a Saturday night dinner at his boss's place when a huge steak is put on his plate. He tucks into the steak along with the vegetables and desert, and as he and his wife are driving home she questions him on his change of diet. She says to him, "What happened to the vegetarian diet?" Gary responds, "It seemed like a good idea at the time!" In other words ideas are temporary concepts which must crystallise into beliefs over time. If forgotten quickly (as most are) they never develop into beliefs.

In conversations, presentations at work or at church, reading and other forms of intellectual stimulation, we are exposed to many ideas. Some of these ideas are repugnant to us and are easily rejected. Others resonate with pressing issues in our lives and ministry, and we enthusiastically embrace them and express them in conversations at that time. However, months later, when a related subject comes up for conversation, we make no reference to these previous ideas because they have been quickly forgotten. Although we may have strongly defended them months before, like the RAM on the computer, they are quickly erased from our memories. It is as if we believe them for a short time (like in the parable of the sower), but they are not beliefs, only ideas.

Core Beliefs

Core beliefs are the beliefs that are held at a subconscious level which we access intuitively. They are like the default settings on my computer. They are pre-set so that every time I turn the computer on the same thing shows on the screen. These are the belief systems I default to whenever I am under stress.

Let me use another food example. In the past I went to see a dietician to understand the nature of foods. I learnt what foods were good for me and what foods I should avoid. In particular I learnt the positive and negative attributes of sugar, salt and fat. I walked out of the consultation feeling much wiser for the discussion and armed with the knowledge as to what I should and shouldn't eat. I now held new ideas and beliefs and was persuaded if I ate according to this information I would undoubtedly lose weight and not put it back on again.

A few weeks later I had a particularly difficult day in the church office consisting of a combination of stressful interviews and disturbing telephone calls. When lunchtime came I knew exactly what I needed. I knew if I had a meat pie with tomato sauce and a large milkshake I would feel a lot better. As I walked from my office to the sandwich shop there was a conflict between my ideas and beliefs.

For many years I have used food as a means of providing comfort rather than sustenance, and under stress I'd defaulted to my core belief. The meat pie and milkshake were fantastic. I felt a lot better and looked forward to the afternoon with enthusiasm. My desire to feel better had overcome my need to lose weight. I had substituted a short term gain for a long term gain, something I would live to regret.

Sources of Core Beliefs

This brings us to a discussion of where these subconscious beliefs come from. Again let me remind you that I am not a psychologist or therapist and so what I am presenting below lacks the weight of scholarship. However, in its simplicity I believe it's a helpful way of understanding where core beliefs come from.

1. Information

This book is not about diets but the formation of Christian leaders, and so I will set aside discussions about where people's eating habits come from. People's religious beliefs stem from three primary sources of information.

a. Their initial belief systems are formed through some **process of discipleship**. This, in certain religious traditions, takes the form of a catechism instruction period. My wife, for example, grew up in the Lutheran church and can still recall her period of being taught Luther's catechism in preparation for her confirmation within the church. This was a foundation being laid as to what she should believe for the rest of her life. Many churches do not have the rite of confirmation. They do however, have classes of discipleship. I remember when I was a young

Christian being taken through a series of courses written by the Navigator movement and Campus Crusade for Christ. I was taught what I should believe about the Bible, evangelism, prayer, fellowship and other such Christian essentials. The people who taught these discipleship courses became influential in the formation of my early religious beliefs.

b. Also powerfully influential are the **generally held religious opinions** of the denomination to which one first belongs. I am greatly thankful for the fact that I spent the early years of my Christian experience within the evangelical tradition of the Anglican church. This involved regularly hearing sound biblical preaching, attending conferences, camps, and a youth group where biblical teaching was taught to me each Sunday.

During this period I was taught what to believe and what not to believe. Forty years later I still draw on this heritage and find little in it that I would want to reject. I have however, found good reasons to augment this sound foundation as my spiritual journey took me into the world of cross-cultural missions and the world of the Christian supernatural, which I did not encounter attending an urban church in a major city.

c. A third major source of the formation of our core belief systems is the **theological education we receive**. Although as a layman I had undertaken part time theological studies, it was not until I undertook full time theological studies that I realised the shallowness of my theological frameworks. Over more than 20 years as a Christian I had gathered many random theological truths but during my theological studies these ideas began to form into a coherent framework on which I could rely for years of future ministry.

The development of this theological framework involved integrating my evangelical heritage through studying people like George

Elden Ladd, Herman Ridderbos and others, from within the conservative evangelical tradition. But my experience of the supernatural, particularly healings and miracles, meant that charismatic theologians such as J Rodman Williams also contributed to what I would call an integrated theological structure.

In the mid 1970's when I undertook my first theological degree, the Pentecostalist movement was just beginning to engage in rigorous theological reflection. For me personally it was enormously stimulating to be able to study in an environment where that early reflection was taking place. But I also appreciated the opportunity of doing post- graduate studies in an evangelical environment, rather than a charismatic environment. Many years later I'm aware just how much these two periods of theological study have influenced the theological beliefs to which I turn intuitively.

2. Formative relationships

As much as discipleship and theological learning form our beliefs, it is also true that formative relationships have a considerable impact on what we believe. The faith, or lack of faith, of parents has a profound impact on the development of children. The belief system of one's first significant Christian leader also has a powerful impact upon us. Because of our respect for the leader we seem to be able to naturally absorb their belief systems, not just what they say but what they are.

The apostle Paul speaks of how people can learn from modelling their lives on his. In 2 Thessalonians 3:9 he speaks of offering himself as a model that they might follow his example (see also 1 Cor 11:1).

A spouse can often also be a powerful source of belief systems. My wife comes from a family that from generation to generation over hundreds of years, has had a deep faith and commitment to the church. I, on the other hand, grew up in a family where religious convictions were personal (if held at all) and there was no visible loyalty to the church. Frequently, in the early years of our marriage, I found myself asking my wife what it was like to grow up in a Christian family as we began the task of being Christian parents ourselves. Jeanie's Germanic Lutheran rural upbringing had been very structured and was very formal and traditional, whereas my upbringing had been non-religious and very liberal.

Most of us have grown up in a highly literate society where reading has also become a major source of the formation of our theological ideas. In this process we develop relationships with particular religious writers. They might be historic figures like Augustine, John Calvin or Martin Luther, alternatively they may be contemporary writers like Philip Yancy or John Stott. Alternatively, if you were born into a Pentecostal tradition they might be Smith Wigglesworth or Kenneth Hagin. These people, through their writings, influence us and it is easy to develop a loyalty to the writer and accept all their opinions uncritically.

3. Experience

In seminary, I was taught to interpret the Bible using sound principles. I studied books on 'Exegesis' and 'Hermeneutics' such as Bernard Ramm's book, *Protestant Biblical Interpretation*, and I try as best as I can to adhere to their sound principles.

However, I am not just a student of the New Testament I am also a human being. The formation of my core beliefs is also influenced by my experience and at times by the absence of experience. An example of this would be what I believe about healing. In my years of formation as an evangelical there was no mention of healing or the healing ministry. But there was considerable teaching about prayer. I learnt to believe that if I love someone I should pray for them in their time of need. I did not have a doctrine of healing but I did have a doctrine and experience of prayer. When I encountered the charismatic movement in the early 1970s I began to hear teaching about healing and was present at meetings when the sick were prayed for. In that I observed instances of healing through the prayers of others, and subsequently in response to my own prayer, my experience of God expanded to include the possibility of healing. In this context I was also given a theology of healing that had been passed down from generation to generation within Pentecostal circles.

However, it did not take me long to realise that despite a theology of healing, the experience in both charismatic and Pentecostal churches is that 'the rhetoric is not always matched by the reality'. The experience of healing, and many times the lack of it, caused me to question both my evangelical theological frameworks and the frameworks which Pentecostalism was presenting to me.

When encountering a leader whose beliefs are different to my own, I have learnt to seek to understand where the beliefs come from. I have reason to question the simple statement "I believe this is what the Bible teaches" as a full and truthful statement of the source of a person's beliefs. I recognise that in exploring deep belief systems I am touching the teaching of people who are deeply respected. I am examining formative relationships and people they have trusted and have been profoundly influenced by. And I am also engaging with a lifetime of experience that needs to be respected. Many of the beliefs, which come from these sources, are sound and are to be respected.

However, some need to be challenged. These may be theological in nature or may be beliefs about themselves. These may be beliefs about how a church should be run or about how a leader relates to those they are leading. They may be beliefs about strategies of ministry or they may be beliefs about how one can effectively motivate others for ministry.

Leadership is about influence, and as a leader I have to accept the fact that it is my role to influence the beliefs of others. If I am unwilling to accept this role, then I ought not to occupy the position of leader.

It is not enough to change the way people feel. Nor is it enough to engage in discussions that may or may not influence the way people think and the ideas they hold. As a leader it is my role to influence what people believe.

> Strategies for Modifying Belief Systems

When I, as a leader, am convinced that the behaviour of someone I am trying to influence is based on flawed beliefs, then I seek to
modify those beliefs. Below are a number of strategies I have found
helpful in this process of modification.

>> Using processes rather than events

Recently I was reading *The Critical Journey*,[12] which is about the
stages of growth of faith that people go through. In the book the
authors observe that as Christians we are on a journey rather than
on a trip. This is quite an interesting distinction. On a trip we know
where we are leaving and where we want to arrive and when. At the
end of a trip there is a sense of satisfaction of having accomplished
our planning and having reached our goal.

The authors observe that the nature of the journey of faith is not
like this. It is rather a journey we are taking where the destination is
known but the focus is on the experience of the journey rather than
simply reaching the destination.

Changing someone's belief system is rarely achieved by requiring
them to undertake a course of study or to attend a particular event.
They may do what you ask and come back and tell you about the
course or the event and what they feel or think. However, this rarely
changes what they fundamentally believe.

In the process of belief modification such input needs to be re-
inforced. They will need to see the new ideas at work and be able to
observe others implementing these ideas, particularly by people
they respect.

In Part B, where I set out a pathway for leadership development,
I define a process rather than a series of unrelated events. The missionary journeys that Jesus initiated for his disciples should not be
seen as events in isolation but rather as parts of a process for their
development. Jesus knew these mission trips would challenge the disciples' pre-existing belief systems. And he also knew that such trips

---

12 Hagberg, J O. and Guelich, R O. *The Critical Journey*. Sheffield Publishing, 1995.

would be only part of a broader process to prepare them for their ministry to come. By the time his disciples reached Caesarea Philippi, where Peter confessed that Jesus is the Christ, they had observed Jesus' ministry, at close hand, and were engaged in ministry themselves.

But their beliefs about the nature of the kingdom of God were still flawed and it would take the death and resurrection of Jesus to significantly modify their beliefs. Even after the resurrection of Jesus and the day of Pentecost, the apostles still seemed bound to a belief that Jesus was only the Messiah of the Jews. Another step in the process of belief modification was necessary. The conversion of Cornelius and his household, while Peter is preaching, further continues the process of their belief system development. It is little wonder therefore that we need to recognise that it will take a process, involving events, rather than a specific event or conversation to significantly impact someone's belief system.

Using case studies rather than exegesis

I believe that local churches should provide consistent opportunities for members to be exposed to sound theological education. Weekly Bible studies and night courses are an important part of the development of sound biblical belief systems. However, in the case of Christian leaders, who have often undertaken theological studies either formally or informally over many years, I have found that a small group which considers case studies is a powerful tool in bringing to light faulty belief systems.

The purpose of such case studies is to create a context in which the members of the group engage in a process of determining what needs to be done in a given set of circumstances. As the leader of the case study group I am concerned to learn not just what they would do, in these circumstances, but to understand the beliefs which lie behind the choices they would make. When each member of the group has had opportunity to respond to the case study, I then model to the group how I myself would go about leading in the particular context and how what I believe has influenced the decisions I would make. An example of such a case study would be the following.

Assume you are the leader of the youth ministry of the church. One Saturday afternoon you are driving home from playing soccer and decide that you will pop into the church to pick up something you have accidentally left behind. You park in the church parking lot and enter through the back of the building using your keys for the church facilities. As you walk down the corridor of the church offices you realise that someone else is in the building. You realise it is the assistant youth leader Brian talking to a 15 year old female member of the youth group. All the lights in the building are off except for a small light which acts as a reading lamp on Brian's desk. As you walk past the office, they are seated on the lounge holding hands. What do you do?

The point of the case study is to place the participants in a real life context that will expose whether or not they are able to apply biblical principles in real life situations. In the case study given above, the members of the case study group differ as to what should be done based on their gender, age or previous experience. The case study is not about finding out the correct things to do. It is about discovering the beliefs of the group members as they indicate the action they would propose to take. It is also about them learning how the decision should be based, not on feelings but on sound beliefs. When finally I, as the case group leader, outline what I would do and why, the level of discussion sometimes moves from action to belief.

Identifying the source and reliability of people's beliefs

I recently heard a Christian leader giving a novel exposition of John 15. In preparing to give this talk the presenter had not studied biblical commentaries but rather historic studies on vineyards in biblical times. It led him to conclude that in John 15:2 Jesus did not say "Every branch in me that does not bear fruit he takes away", but rather "every branch in me that does not bear fruit he lifts up". In doing this he argued that the Greek verb 'airo' translated commonly as 'takes away', is equally validly translated as lift (see Matt 4:6).

My initial reaction was one of concern that he would feel able to overthrow the translation of this verb used by most respected translators. What interested me more was from where he got the idea. I asked him "Did you get the idea from a commentary?", and he said "No! I didn't read any commentaries in preparing for the talk". But he then acknowledged that the idea had come from someone else who he'd heard preaching many years ago. This was helpful because I had now identified the source of this belief and was able to consider whether or not it was a reliable source.

Before challenging the belief itself it was important for me to find from whom the belief had originally come. If this source was someone the leader highly respected, I needed to understand that I was not just challenging a belief but a relationship.

I realise that often people do not even recall from where a particular belief has come. But in the case of biblical beliefs, such as the example given above, people normally do remember where they originally got the idea.

Once I have identified the source of belief as being derived from someone who is highly respected, it becomes necessary to challenge the belief with great care. Few of us would view ourselves as being infallible and so all those we look up to need to be seen as having ideas which are capable of being challenged.

Where such a person has been a long term positive influence, it is important not to undermine the person's influence which could damage many of the positive beliefs which they have imparted to the person you are trying to help. But if the beliefs are flawed they need to be gently challenged whilst respecting the source from which they have come.

Allowing pragmatism to ask the questions rather than give the answers

We live in a world where some Christians have a second canon which has been described as 'what works'. Because of this Christian leaders go to conferences which offer them a diet of how to do certain things successfully. In this context sometimes the ends justify the means. In this case pragmatism gives the answers rather than asks the questions.

What I prefer to do is use pragmatic issues to pose the questions and to move from those questions to the text of Scripture. Where a belief is flawed there will be a divergence between what seems to work, in a pragmatic sense, and what the Scripture says. This will mean one of two things. Either the perception of what works is wrong because the leader does not fully understand all the issues involved, or alternatively their understanding of what the Scripture teaches needs to be modified.

I have used the lack of healing at Pentecostal gatherings to challenge some leaders' beliefs as to what the Scriptures teach about healing. But I have also used the experience of healing to challenge the beliefs of those who are cessationists. As a leader I have often been challenged to ask myself questions based on the apparent mythologies of traditions of which I would find myself strongly in sympathy. If I start the process merely arguing with someone as to what they believe the Bible says, it inevitably ends with not what the Bible says but what the Bible means and the dispute becomes one of hermeneutics. Where, however, I am able to start with a pragmatic issue and turn it into a question, I find we often go to the Scripture with a different spirit of humility both seeking to learn. This only becomes 'interpreting Scripture by experience' if one's experience, or lack of it, gives the answer rather than asks the question.

Expanding the sources of influence

It is very difficult for a leader to change his or her faulty belief systems from a position of isolation. Isolation is not just a matter of where one lives but who one meets with. Developing leaders change their beliefs incrementally. It is bad for the leader and bad for the group they are leading if there are huge fluctuations in the beliefs of the leader. Sometimes a leader becomes isolated so that everyone who influences him or her holds all the same ideas and beliefs. In such a case it is difficult for such leaders to expand their beliefs in ways that leadership may require.

In this I am not talking about rejecting sound and long held belief systems. I am referring to the ability to expand one's understanding of life in the Kingdom as one's leadership role becomes more and more complex or when the context of leadership changes significantly.

Many years ago I was approached by someone graduating from a well known and respected Bible college who was going to Africa as a missionary. This person was a mature Christian and had received an excellent theological education at the institution she had attended.

However, previous missionaries who had returned from the area where this person was going had experienced extreme emotional oppression such that in two or three cases there had been a serious emotional and psychological breakdown. The person was going to a part of Africa known for spiritual darkness, witchcraft and the demonic. And yet the person's theological training had made few references to the kinds of things that she was going to encounter.

I received the call because my wife and I had recently returned from three years ministering in the Fijian Islands, amongst Hindus, and stories of the kind of situations we had found ourselves in had begun to circulate. The person who rang me asked if I could share more of these experiences with her and share what I had learned about spiritual darkness and dealing with the demonic. Nothing I shared challenged the biblical beliefs she had been taught in Bible college. What I said merely took her into an area that had not been covered at all.

I can think of other instances where I have been consulted by people from a charismatic or Pentecostal background where the questions they have raised have led me to suggest they read a series of non-Pentecostal authors to make up deficiencies in their Bible or theological training.

The point being that belief systems at times need expanding rather than amending. What people believe is not wrong, but neither is it complete. Many religious traditions find this possibility hard to accept.

Deepening a person's sense of historical perspective

An old adage states that those who are ignorant of history are bound to repeat its mistakes. And yet enthusiastic young leaders often assume that the situations they face are new. In modifying a person's beliefs it is often helpful to present to that person an historic perspective on the development of their wrongly-held beliefs.

For example in developing a sound biblical view of the integration of faith and life in the workplace I have often encouraged people to read some of the literature from the period of the Puritans. The Puritans, of the Victorian era, developed a bad name and yet it is from puritan teaching that the Protestant work-ethic derives.

Similarly in confronting contemporary leaders as to their beliefs about issues such as prosperity, I have drawn the attention of the leaders to the anti-Semitism of the church in the second century when the divide between the church and Judaism occurred. I have encouraged them to not view the Old Testament in isolation from the New and conversely not to deal with the New Testament in isolation from the Old. For some people, deepening a sense of historical perspective allows them to modify beliefs that are derived from some present minister who they greatly respect but who may represent only one historical perspective.

Giving a motivation for change

As a Christian leader change is not an option but a lifestyle. Our beliefs must change and develop. Many foundational beliefs must not change for they are the foundation of the gospel and of our ministries. But other beliefs that relate to styles and methods of ministry, will need to change over time. We live in a culture which has largely disciplined mistakes and not rewarded success. In this kind of culture most leaders are reluctant to change their beliefs for fear of being disciplined. It is helpful to find ways of rewarding people who show a willingness to grow and develop even if it means changing some beliefs which they have held on to for a long period of time.

Conclusion

In writing this chapter I have used commonly held belief systems encountered in my own personal spiritual journey. Along the way I may have touched some raw nerves to do with issues you may 'feel' strongly about or subjects where you have 'strong ideas'. It is not my intention to persuade you as to my own beliefs, or the beliefs of the movement to which I belong. These illustrations were given simply to highlight the significance of belief systems within the life of leaders.

What I have sought to do is to point out that the 'L' factor of leadership includes the belief system of the leader. And that in developing leaders we have to accept that one of our roles is to tackle these belief systems and to ensure that the beliefs of the leader are consistent with the beliefs of the organisation which they are being asked to lead.

For you this may mean that you are trying to lead in the wrong context. Your foundational beliefs are inconsistent with the belief system of the organisation you have been asked to serve. Alternatively it may have confronted you with the fact that you will need to change the beliefs of those who are around you before you are able to effectively lead the organisation.

It is a reminder to us also that many programmes we may choose to borrow and integrate into our own churches reflect the beliefs of those who have designed them. Although such programmes may work in another context they may do great damage in our own church if the programmes reflect a belief system inconsistent with our own. For this reason most programmes will need to be adapted rather than adopted.

This also helps us to understand why some leaders with 'intellectual firepower' are inflexible. It is because of their beliefs as opposed to their intellectual capacity.

CHAPTER FIVE
COMPLEXITY

A s stated earlier, the three elements of The 'L' Factor, are:

1. intellectual strength;
2. a sound belief system (strongly held beliefs); and
3. the capacity to deal with increasing complexity.

I have elected to discuss the first two elements in some depth in the first part of the book. However, the third element I shall discuss comprehensively in Part B.

Coping with complexity in organisations is a critical ability because leadership is tri-dimensional. It is not only about me and those I lead. It is also about what we are trying to do in the context in which we are serving.

As one progresses up the leadership ladder of an organisation, the nature of what one is asked to do changes in the same way ministry roles evolve. A common denominator in this change is that the roles become more and more complex in two dimensions. The number of things the leader has to think about (at the same time) multiplies — like the proverbial juggler. And the length of time which the leader is required to focus elongates.

Most people can cope with focussing on one thing for a short period of time. Like leading a small group for an hour and a half a week. But most people will struggle leading a large church with a 10 year plan!

The implications of this capacity, and the presence of different capacities for coping with complexity, shall form the basis of Chapter 7 in Part B.

CHAPTER SIX
EMOTIONAL INTELLIGENCE (EQ)

A number of recent authors of leadership books, like Alistair Mant[13] have recognised that the absence of 'emotional intelligence' can disqualify a person from being an effective leader. Despite the presence of good judgment, a sound belief system and a capacity for coping with complexity, emotional issues may seriously impede a person's progress in their leadership formation and development.

In some organisations what is known as EQ has become the final determinant as to whether a person gets a senior leadership position or not. Many people with intellectual strength, sound belief systems and a capacity for complexity, want jobs so it becomes necessary to distinguish them by other means. Such high performance organisations place a high value on teams and teamwork. They also don't want to lose good managers and leaders because of emotionally damaged executives.

Family businesses started by the family patriarch, have frequently suffered from this problem. The 'old man' frustrates and abuses any manager who shows good leadership potential, thus, family companies rarely survive more than two generations.

Churches started by strong gifted leaders (with serious emotional flaws) have often suffered the same fate. As a consequence the earlier it is possible to identify areas of EQ which need looking into, and working through, the better. I recommend a six monthly assessment of a leader's performance based not just on task competence, but also on emotional intelligence. I have included as an appendix a leadership evaluation form which should be completed by both

---

13 Mant, A. *Intelligent Leadership*. Allen & Unwin, 1997.

the person being evaluated and the person to whom they are accountable. Its content is based on the book, *Working with Emotional Intelligence.*[14] However, it has been created to reflect biblical values and work in the context of Christian ministry.

As Christian leaders the need exists to resource competencies outside of ourselves. In this area medical doctors, psychologists and counsellors can become trainers of leaders as much as those who are skilled in strategic planning or systems design. The damage currently occurring to the church by sexual predators in clergy clothing, in part derives from the fact that ministry giftedness has been allowed for many years to blind authorities to serious moral and emotional breakdowns.

Knowing what emotionally damaged leaders can do one can only wonder how long it will be before the spiritually and emotionally abused members of churches begin to speak out in the same way as those who have been sexually abused.

I have included in the Suggested Reading list, a brief bibliography on this important subject.

---

14 Goleman, D. *Working With Emotional Intelligence.* Bloomsbury, 1998.

DEVELOPING LEADERS

CHAPTER SEVEN

LEVELS OF LEADERSHIP

Diagram 7.1: The Leadership Development Path

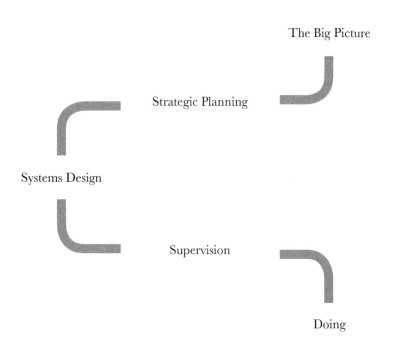

The Big Picture

Strategic Planning

Systems Design

Supervision

Doing

The Reverend Graham White sat at his desk considering a problem that had been recurring in the 15 years of his ministry at St Gregory's, South London. The church was a large evangelical Anglican parish that was led by him and a staff team of six. In his team was an assistant ordained minister, a part-time music director, a full time youth worker, a part-time children's worker and a secretary/administrator. Over the years in both the children's and youth area there had been a turnover of staff approximately every three to four years, and he recognised that this change of leadership seemed to be directly related to the fact that these areas of ministry, though vital, had not experienced significant growth.

This was in direct contrast to the services of the church that had gone from two, when the rector joined the parish, to six per Sunday. These services had introduced elements of creative ministry including a strong drama team and contemporary music ministry. In recent years multi- media resources (such as PowerPoint) had been introduced into the services which meant that the services were both relevant and effective.

As he sat reading a letter of resignation from the children's church worker he experienced a feeling he'd felt many times before. He was confident that God would provide someone to lead this ministry which was critical for the retention of young families in the church. There was also the feeling of mild desperation as to who he could find to perform the task. He called his assistant Bruce to his office and the following conversation ensued:

Rev Graham: Please read this letter and then we need to discuss it.

Bruce: I guess this comes as no surprise as Kathy seemed to be going nowhere in her ministry and has been expressing a lack of confidence in her ability to lead the ministry.

Rev Graham: Why is it that leaders of the children's ministry and youth areas seem to get discouraged where in other areas we are able to retain leaders for a long period of time? Do you think it's the people we choose or is there something inherently different in these areas of ministry which seems to make it so hard?

Bruce: Well I'm not sure but I remember recently at a leadership seminar hearing leadership being described as tri-dimensional. When I first heard this I thought 'Oh no, surely life can't be that complex'. But when it was explained, I realised that leadership does have three dimensions. There is the dimension of the leader, there is the dimension of those who the leader is leading) and there is the context in which the leadership takes place. The seminar presenter also indicated that because of the reality of tri-dimensional leadership, leaders in different contexts require different kinds of support so that in mentoring leaders it is not right for the senior leader to use one leadership style with all the leaders under him or her.

Rev Graham: Are you saying that it's my fault? That I'm effective in supporting leaders in some areas of ministry but ineffective in other areas? Surely I can't be an authority in everything? In fact I feel the longer I am in ministry the less I know about specific ministry areas.

Bruce: No, that's not what I'm saying. But what I think I am beginning to learn is that leaders need to take a leadership pathway of development and that we have a responsibility to create such pathways and to support developing leaders as they journey along that pathway. I guess you and I are going to choose someone to lead the children's work without really knowing whether or not that person will be competent to lead. I think our history of decision making, when it comes to staff appointments, is probably best described as making decisions in a crisis rather than as part of a process.

Rev Graham: I think it's time for us to pray for surely God has someone who can fill this position.

Identification of Leader's Potential

For someone who has lead the same church for almost 20 years I have to confess that I have been in the situation described above many times. Recognising the stress it placed on me and other key leaders we sought a better way. I was attracted to the concept of all key leaders having an assistant who was in a sense being trained to take over the role if the senior leader for some reason, had to step down.

I was also attracted to a concept of four levels of leadership in each ministry area. This concept was based on the way the military operates in times of war, which ensured that if there was a casualty within the ranks of officers there was always someone to take over. Sergeants became Lieutenants, Lieutenants became Captains, Captains became Majors and so on.

Both of these concepts still appeal to me, however, I have come to realise that they are static in nature. For example, once an assistant leader is in place they remain in place in that position for as long as the leader they are serving continues in their position. My experience has been that often when the leader chooses to step down their assistant does the same thing, as a strong relationship has been forged between the two. So that rather than providing someone to take over, I have been left in the situation where I have to find both a leader and an assistant leader.

The same can be said for the concept of four **depths** of leadership in a church. These depths frequently involve:
1. depth two being a member of staff;
2. depth three being a senior lay leader; and
3. depth four being a relatively new lay leader.

I am now of the opinion that these should not be individual people but groups of people so that there is a pool from which to choose in appointing people to senior or more complex levels of leadership. However, the problem still exists whereby, particularly in the top two depths, that kind of structure can be in place for extended periods of time. In recognising the limitations of these two approaches I have come to believe that a process of leadership development yields the best long term results. In the material that follows I seek to outline the kind of understanding necessary to develop such a process. Whether a church is large (eg, has a staff of six or more) or is smaller, (has a staff of one), the same principles apply in developing a helpful process.

In essence what I'm saying is that the time comes when we must move from the identification of a leader's potential — the 'born' factor, to the 'made' process.

In the first part of this book I have sought to discuss different indicators which would suggest that a person has leadership potential. I discussed the need for intellectual strength, well established, sound beliefs, and the capacity for sound judgment. As mentioned under the title 'The Big Picture' there is another factor which relates to **the capacity of a leader to handle complexity**.

In leadership theory writers have recognised that in all organisations there are stratas of complexity which relate to a combination of the number of issues needing to be considered and the length of time over which those decisions will have an impact. Most of the literature related to this concept is highly complex. I will attempt to simplify it for you.

What is significant for the purposes of this discussion is that these stratas, which have been identified, are stepping stones in the process whereby leaders are made and not just born.

There is a built-in assumption that leaders ought never be allowed to jump from one strata to two or three stratas above, irrespective of the excellence of their performance at the level at which they are currently functioning. This is because each of the stratas is a developmental stage in which a leader can actually develop skills which will be needed in the next strata. Leaders of high potential may move through the stratas relatively quickly but no strata should be omitted from the development path of a leader.

From here on I have chosen to refer to them as 'levels' rather than 'stratas' though the concept is the same.

Diagram 7.1 (p43) identifies five levels of leadership development. However, I prefer to see them as places of leadership development. By this I mean they are a context in which someone may develop new skills and expand existing ones. In very large organisations there can be up to eight such levels but I have yet to encounter a church which has had more than five.

Understanding How the Leadership Task Changes in Organisations

I want to now briefly discuss each of the five levels of development normally encountered in churches so that you get a general sense of why each level is different. I will take each of the five levels of leadership and describe the nature of the tasks performed at each one. It is critical to understand that at each level there is greater complexity and ambiguity.

By this I mean two things.

Firstly, the number of tasks undertaken multiply. Secondly, the length of time to be considered by the leader elongates. Some tasks are just complex. Others are both complex and ambiguous.

> Level One: Doing

Bronwyn McDonald leads a cell group in the life of her local church. In this role she is assisted by an assistant cell leader and by a couple who host the meeting. Her brother Jim also plays guitar to accompany the singing which is part of the regular life of the cell group. Bronwyn's leadership role involves interacting with her assistant, her hosts and her brother. The task fundamentally doesn't change from week to week and the impact of any decisions she makes rarely lasts longer than two or three months.

For Bronwyn it is her first opportunity to be a leader. She accepted the position with fear and trembling but, after a short period, has begun to enjoy the experience of influencing others, the heart of leadership. Initially she found planning the weekly programmes stressful and working with the other members of her team challenging, however the repetitive nature of her leadership task allowed her to develop in a context where mistakes could be made without hugely negative consequences. Her cell group supervisor kept in constant contact in   the first few months and was able to provide answers to any questions which arose.

Under her leadership the cell has doubled over a period of 18 months and she is now facing the possibility of the group dividing to become two cells with her assistant leading one while she leads the other.

Her only disappointment is that her best friend Judy also began to lead a group at the same time but, after three months, stepped down after experiencing migraine headaches during meeting days.

> Level Two: Supervision

Rodney Brown was Bronwyn's supervisor. Three years ago he had been asked to lead his first cell group. He had been part of the cell life of his church for a number of years since the time of his conversion to Christ. He had spent two years as an assistant leader in the group which he subsequently took over. Under his leadership of the group he had been able to effectively develop the ministry potential of a number of people in the group. The cell, having stagnated for two or three years, had now grown under his innovative leadership and he had effectively chosen and developed another assistant leader.

His own group's numbers had doubled and at the time of his handing over its leadership to become a supervisor, it was ready to become two separate groups.

When he was asked to become a cell group supervisor he had mixed feelings. He really enjoyed leading his cell group. He loved helping others to realise their ministry potential and he loved direct contact with people. On the other hand he had himself experienced the value of an effective supervisor when he first started out as a cell leader.

Like Bronwyn he had a friend who had also been a cell leader but who had quit with feelings of frustration and disappointment. He sensed that his friend had not had a supervisor like the one he had worked with. He could see that an effective supervisor didn't just help people develop their **ministry potential** but was vital in helping people develop their **leadership potential**.[15] Somewhat reluctantly therefore, he resigned his role as a cell group leader and became a supervisor of eight cell groups.

When he was leading a cell group he had only three other people who looked to him for leadership. Now that he was a supervisor there were eight cell leaders who would ring him from time to time seeking advice. He also had the responsibility of calling each one of them on a monthly basis to provide a combination of support and accountability. No longer did he find himself thinking from week to week or for just a few months in advance. He found that he needed to develop an annual strategy involving getting his group of leaders together for training. He also needed to monitor the identification and development of assistant group leaders so that a pool of potential cell leaders would be available when either cell leaders needed to step down or new groups needed to form.

To his surprise he found the role of supervising more complex than the role of leading a group.

When leading a cell he felt he often needed to have three or four balls in the air like a juggler. But now it seemed six or seven needed to be in the air. At times he also felt that there were two or three lying on the ground.

To make matters worse he soon discovered that each of the cell leaders he was supervising were at different levels of development as a leader and that he needed to match his supervision style to their

---

15 In hindsight it is clear I did not sufficiently stress in *The Empowered Church* that 'ministry' is not inferior to 'leadership'. Many outstanding teachers, for example, decline promotion and sacrifice salary increases, when offered leadership roles within the organisation reflecting this value.

maturity levels. His preferred style was merely to delegate and trust the person to whom the role was delegated. This was effective sometimes, at other times, it wasn't.

He soon found the need to discuss these issues with his previous supervisor who gave him a helpful model to work with. He was told that maturity in leadership is a combination of confidence, ability and willingness. He was also told to identify which of these three areas may be lacking in any particular leader or, in some cases, to recognise that more than one factor may be present. He was advised that this would help him in identifying the difference he could make by adopting appropriate supervisory styles.

He also needed training in strategic planning. He drew great comfort from the fact that the other three cell group supervisors were also performing similar tasks. When they met together, quarterly, he found the training on strategic planning particularly helpful and access to group training material was also essential. What he also benefited from was access to level three leaders. Interaction between level two and level three leaders is an important part of the process of developing someone as they move down the pathway of leadership development.

> Level Three: Leadership of Systems

Jonathan Haig was the director of cell groups in the church, and was working for the church one day a week. Jonathan had been effective as a cell group leader and as a small group supervisor. Three years earlier the previous cell group director had been asked to become the missions director of the church and Jonathan had been asked to take her place.

He had benefited from her input. He knew the benefits the role provided to both the supervisors and cell group leaders and how important the cell life was to the overall wellbeing of the church. He was beginning to sense a potential call to full time ministry and after two years as a supervisor was feeling ready for a challenge.

He didn't really understand what was involved in being the director of the cell group ministry but assumed it was probably simply a further extension of what he had done as a cell leader and a supervisor. He could not have been more wrong!

What he didn't realise was that this level of leadership (level three) involves a significantly different kind of leadership. Both levels one and two are heavily focused on relating to people.

Whilst level three involves the director relating to supervisors, **the primary nature of the role shifts from a people focus to a systems focus**. Soon after becoming the cell groups' director he was called into the office of the associate pastor. David, to whom he now reported, made the simple statement, "I think our cell group system is becoming stale and needs a complete overhaul". David told him to continue to run the present system as it was, but to spend the first few months as director focussing on researching what other churches were doing in small group or cell life.

He was given a budget for small groups and sent to a small groups conference.

At the end of three months' research, he was to then spend the next three months reviewing the church's cell group system and, if necessary, come up with the design for a process to implement a completely new cell group system.

He was told that he should anticipate the new cell group system would last for between three to five years and that he should take into account the fact that the adaptation of the new system would probably take 12 months to implement and may not be fully functioning until the second or even the third year.

He was told that, in strategic planning, he had to think at least three years ahead and his focus was to be 'systems' and not 'people'.

This was all a bit of a shock! He realised that organisations had systems but to him they were like the atmosphere. They were there, had a significant role, but were largely unseen and simply taken for granted. Knowing that he would miss contact with people he ensured that he and his wife belonged to a cell group; a group of which he was not the leader. He also maintained regular contact with the team of supervisors.

He soon made a discovery. In the church there were four other people who led areas of ministry. He discovered that each of them had a role similar to his own. These leaders were concerned with systems and he found that he benefited greatly as he met with these people to talk about the designing, implementation and maintenance of systems. He also found, to his surprise, that a friend of his in a senior management role in a large corporation became a great source of help and information to him. He found that his friend had been required to regularly go to seminars for training in systems development, and figured out that he might not get this training within the context of the church.

As part of the first three months in the role he did significant reading of small group literature, most of which however was written for small group leaders not for small group ministry directors.

He went to a small groups conference but much to his disappointment the focus was on the content of small group Bible studies, worship in the context of small groups and small group leadership.

None of the electives offered dealt with cell group system design. After some digging he found that such literature did exist but that training to be a 'systems' leader, in the context of small groups, was rarely available.

He enrolled in a course on systems design at an evening college for management development. He found that three months was not enough to do the research and it was only after 12 months that he was ready to hand his boss David, a draft proposal for the implementation of a new cell group system.

It took six months for the proposal to be reviewed and approved (after some modification) and that implementation took a further 12 months. At the end of a period of three years on the job he was now seeing the fruit of his role as the designer of a system and was sustained through this lengthy period by the fact that he continued to relate to the supervisors and was himself part of a cell group.

He also realised that neither the cell group leaders or the supervisors really understood what his job was. He wondered about that.[16] The job was far more complex than he had realised. He realised that the director of the children's work had a role similar to his own and that she didn't seem to understand what the role was and that she had been promoted straight from level one to level three without any experience of supervision. As he thought about it, he realised in the children's church the ministry leader seemed to change every few years and he wondered if there was a relationship between this turnover and an inadequate development process for preparing people to be systems leaders.

Between level two and level three, as has been demonstrated, the focus of a leader shifts from people to organisational issues.

> Level Four: Strategic Planning

Barbara had been in the church for 15 years. After a few years of sitting in the pews, she had joined a cell group and within 12 months had become an assistant cell group leader. After a further 12 months she had been given the leadership of a small group which had flourished. She had then been asked to become a small group supervisor and had fulfilled that role for a period of three years. Much to her surprise two years later she had been called to the senior pastor's office for a meeting. She had assumed that there was to be a change in the small group structure and that she was going to be offered the role of director of small group ministries.

However, the pastor advised her that they were wanting to start a new department based on an intentionalised discipleship programme in the church. Barbara had accepted the challenge and within three years had built a team involving men, women and youth leaders who were committed to an intentionalised discipleship programme within the life of the church. The effectiveness of the discipleship programme was evident in many areas of the church and as a result,

16 Subsequently he wondered whether the Senior Pastor did either!

after only a short period she had been called again into the senior pastor's office.

Pastor David looked her squarely in the eyes and said, "Barbara I believe God is calling you to full-time service in the church. You have proved yourself to be effective at levels one, two and three of the leadership structure of our church. Initially I would like to offer you a part-time staff position, for two days a week, with a hope that in time it will become full-time. How are your theological studies going?"

Sensing the possibility of such a call Barbara had for a number of years been attending Bible college part-time at night and had completed a diploma in biblical studies. With further work she could convert the diploma into a degree in theology. But the time involved was not possible because of her involvement with family life, work life and the church.

She was surprised to hear the pastor say "Barbara, of the two days a week you will be on the church staff, we expect you to spend half a day a week continuing your theological studies as we require all full-time staff to hold a minimum of an undergraduate degree in theology. We will pay for your educational fees as part of our commitment to your future development".

As she sat there Barbara realised that her pastor still hadn't told her what it was that she was going to be asked to do. She waited to hear what would be said. "Barbara, the executive of the church has decided that we need to start a new church service late Sunday afternoon. It is to be targeted at families with young children and we want you to lead the team which will start this new service". Internally she began to mildly panic. She thought, 'Now hang on a minute. I'm an expert in small groups and discipleship. I know nothing about pioneering and leading new services'. She said to her pastor, "Are you sure I am the right person for this job?"

Her pastor smiled at her and said: "Barbara, you have proved yourself competent as an effective cell group leader, as a supervisor and as a systems designer. All of these skills are pre-requisites to the task we are offering you. Yes, the new role involves skills which you may not currently possess, however, we are committed to training you in these skills and I will be there as your mentor. We will resource you with levels one, two and three leaders drawn from other areas of the ministry of the church. I will connect you with a number of people who have been involved in starting new services. You can learn a lot from others and from literature on church and congregational planting. However, in the end this is an opportunity for you to put your own mark on the church. It is you who will need to develop a strategic plan for the development of the service and all the different ministries which will be associated with it. You will not actively implement those plans. Nor indeed will you design the systems which will be essential for the new service. Competent level three and level two leaders will do this for you.

You will be expected to develop a plan for between three to five years. The plan will incorporate a vision which can be communicated to those we will recruit for you. The plan will have a timeline as to when the service shall start, and shall include a budget for the cost of commencing this service and for its ongoing running. The plan shall include a strategy for attracting people to the service and shall discuss the possible negative impact of the starting of this new service on our existing services".

Barbara pondered the complexity of what she was being asked to accomplish. Now she would be dealing with multiple systems, multiple level leaders, finances, internal church politics and be required to preach regularly. This was something she had begun but in which she lacked confidence. She suspected that hidden in the job were elements she could only discover by doing, and that surprises were likely in store. She also knew she wanted to try and succeed at this new level of leadership.

The shift from level three to level four requires the greatest change in capability. Levels one to three are roles for which data is available to guide decision making. In level four the leader is planning the future and much greater ambiguity exists.

> Level Five: The Big Picture

Richard Black had been leading the evening service at the Villawood Baptist Church for seven years. Under his leadership the service had grown from 80 to 150 and he was ready for a challenge. He had proved effective as a cell group leader, a cell group supervisor and as director of the cell groups ministry of the church. For the past three years he had participated in the executive board of the church and had been mentored by a senior pastor he respected, although they possessed different spiritual gifts and temperaments. The senior pastor was due to retire in six months and the board of the church had invited Richard to apply for the position as the next senior pastor of the church.

Based on his experience at levels one to four in the church he felt confident that he was ready for the next step. He knew the church, shared all its core values, and was known and respected for both his leadership gift and his pastoral and preaching ministry. He did not covet the role but felt that all that had happened in his life to this point was leading in this direction.

The interview had gone well and to nobody's surprise he was offered the position and six months later became the senior pastor of the church. The previous senior pastor of the church, after many years of effective ministry, had gradually tired. Richard knew there were a number of issues in the church which needed attention, and required significant change. This was something the previous pastor had been unable to do. Being new and 20 years younger he felt he had the energy to take up the challenge.

During his first day on the job he spoke to six of the key leaders of the church. By the end of the day he was beginning to have second thoughts and for the first time began to understand the difference between a level four and level five leader.

The first meeting in the morning had been with Kevin the church administrator. Kevin advised him that he was weary from the constant pressure of trying to pay bills month by month when the church had no cash reserves. He had been head hunted by another church in the same denomination which had a policy of maintaining a minimum of two months operating reserves, and he had accepted the new position under the same operating guidelines. He would be leaving in one month.

The second meeting was with Sally the church's music director. Sally advised him that on Sunday night thieves had broken into the main sanctuary and that all the electronic gear stored in the church had been stolen. She said that this had both good and bad implications. The bad part was that they would need to hire gear for a few weeks and there was no money in the budget provided for such an event. The good part was that all the gear was insured and that it would be an opportunity for them to upgrade a number of the pieces of the equipment and that she had a strategic plan in place which required a modernisation of all the church's electronic equipment. She said she knew what was needed but that she would need his support to lobby for these changes with older members of the congregation and with the church's finance board.

The third staff person to arrive was Rosemary the church's children's director. Rosemary closed the door and sat down obviously reluctant to begin what she had to say. After a pause she dropped the following bombshell. "We have a problem in the children's church. It would appear that one of our teachers has been sexually molesting children under his care". She then asked what she should do. Did they need to immediately call in the police? Did they need to call in someone from the church denomination? Who in the church leadership needs to know? Ought she resign?"

Richard sat there stunned, for nothing in his years of experience had prepared him for such an event. However, in the back of his mind was a recollection that another church in his movement had gone through something similar and he knew how to get hold of advice to help his staff member through this difficult situation. He listened carefully and then they arranged an appointment the following day to discuss the matter further.

The fourth person to see him was his wife. She was a part-time staff member of the church involved in leading the women's ministry. The issue she wanted to discuss surprised him. She said, "I've loved working **with you** in the ministry over these years but I'm not sure I want to work **for you**!" Her concern was that being accountable to him in the workplace may put stress on their marriage and family life. She felt that for it to work there needed to be some new boundaries put in place so that the church would not dominate their home or family life and that these issues needed to be faced sooner rather than later.

Interview number five was with the church architect. Unknown to Richard was the fact that the retired senior pastor had, for a number of years, conceived a plan for expanding the church sanctuary. Whilst nothing had been said publicly, architectural drawings had been prepared and a decision was needed as to whether the building extension was to proceed. As he listened to the plan and thought about the needs for the church there was great merit in what was being proposed. However, this would involve Richard for the first time in a process of raising a significant amount of money from the congregation. Although previously he had been required to prepare budgets and to spend money consistent with those budgets the overall finances of the church had always been the responsibility of the senior pastor. In a sense he had never needed to worry whether there would be enough money week to week to run the ministry. The young adult service took offerings but those monies merely disappeared into the overall funds of the church. Whether or not that service could pay its bills or fund its staff, had never been an issue. It was a generous church and cross-subsidisation meant that new ministries could be started whether they were able to be financially sustainable or not in the short term. Now the weight for the overall finances of the church rested squarely on Richard's shoulders, and he felt it.

The last person sitting opposite him was the secretary of the previous senior pastor. Richard did not want a secretary. He wanted a personal assistant, but he wasn't sure what the difference was. Beverley had excellent communication skills, was professional on the telephone, could efficiently maintain a diary and had first rate computer skills. However, Beverley saw this as a job rather than as a ministry, and would arrive at 8.55 am and leave pretty much at 5.00 pm sharp. She had a young family and her husband had a demanding job in industry.

As they sat talking about how they would work together as a team, Richard sensed that Beverley was not the person he needed working with him. He wasn't sure what skills he did need but a friend had a superb personal assistant and he planned to take her to lunch to find out exactly what it was that she did.

Richard also realised that these days, removing someone from a position they have held for a number of years is not easy due to government requirements for the protection of employees. Beverley was competent and committed to what she did, which made what he proposed to do even more difficult. She and her family had been members of the church for many years and he wasn't sure she would understand, as there was prestige associated with being the secretary to the senior pastor.

After talking for a little while, Beverley left and Richard sat back at his desk pondering the 'big picture'.

During the day he had not ministered to anybody. He'd neither taught nor preached. In fact he had done nothing which might be termed 'ministry'. He had experienced for the first time what a level five leader does from day to day. He knew today was not going to be a prototype of each day which lay ahead of him. And he knew that the church was in a period of transition now that he had assumed leadership. Yet he also sensed that these were the kinds of issues he alone would have to face in the years to come on a regular basis.

The complexity of his role had increased again. Now he was expected to think five to 10 years in advance, and though the number of people directly reporting to him had not increased, the diversity of the issues which would be discussed had increased significantly. In time he would also have to look outward and not just deal with internal issues. He would consider external alliances with other organisations and strategic challenges which those focussing on day to day issues rarely ponder. He would need to reflect on the changing culture and demographics surrounding the church and initiate pro-active responses. He would have to oversee a process for the evaluation of the relevance of strategic programmes.

Levels and Church Membership

Churches with active membership under 100 frequently function with pastors at level two or three. Churches between 100 and 250 members frequently have pastors who function at level four. Churches with over 250 adults require leaders at level five. Other Christian institutions, (eg, large theological training colleges), will probably have all five levels but with a smaller number of people at each level. This is because they tend not to have as many volunteers in positions of leadership.

Creating a Leadership Development Pathway

At the beginning of this chapter Diagram 7.1 illustrates a leadership development pathway. Having just described these five levels in narrative form, it is necessary now to turn these levels into a process, rather than to simply see them as job descriptions of people within an organisation.

The difficulty of organisational charts, which simply draw lines and boxes including titles and people's names, is that it is easy to assume that the picture portrayed describes a status quo rather than a dynamic process. For this reason I would invite you as a reader to undertake a task before you read further.

You may discover that in the organisation you lead or are involved in, various job descriptions combine both levels two and three or

On a sheet of paper do a diagrammatic portrayal of the key roles in your organisation based on the five levels of leadership.

levels three and four.

Although a single title is given to the person this is a misnomer. In reality the person is holding different positions at different levels of leadership.

As stated above, if a church has over 250 adult members, it will have all five levels of leadership. However, in many cases the senior pastor combines levels five, four and three frequently due to a reluctance to delegate leadership to others. In the case of a smaller church a leader may combine levels four, three and two, again for the same reason.

It would therefore be helpful for you to view your organisation not based on people, but based on tasks. Two lists may well be required. The first based on titles and names, a second based on tasks. When comparing these two lists it may expose the fact that little systems design work has been done in the organisation, even though there are leaders, supervisors and strategic planners. A simple example of the first list is as follows:

Bill Drake — Senior Pastor

Catherine Bellows — Children's Leader Graeme Chase — Youth Director

Anne Summerset — Aged Visitation Coordinator

An example of the same staff and leaders in the second list might be:

Level four leaders

Strategic planning and visionary — Pastor Bill

Level three (systems) leaders

Children's ministry — Pastor Catherine Youth ministry — Pastor Graeme

Level two leader

Aged care supervisor — Anne

Conversely it may indicate that there is an absence of strategic planning and that the organisation consists of one level five leader and leaders at levels three, two and one.

It will also be helpful to ask the question, in case of levels five and four, as to whether or not they have proven themselves effective at levels one, two and three.[17]

A common mistake made in church planting, by many of the new church movements, is sending people to church plant who have had some experience at levels one and two and have a strong ministry gift of preaching and evangelism. But these people are unproven at level three and higher. It is little wonder that these people can gather a crowd but can't build a church.

An analogy from the business world might be helpful at this point. It is well known that the major employers are not big business but in fact small business. In many ways small business is like the small church of our nation. Small businesses survive on an individual, or perhaps a husband and wife, possessing certain technical skills sufficient to effectively run the small business. This person does not necessarily possess levels three, four or five leadership skills so their businesses remain small. The same is true of small churches.

This begs the question as to what comes first. Does a church need to become large before it can develop a leadership pathway? Alternatively, will the development of a leadership pathway result in a church becoming larger? I am in no doubt that the second situation is the case. In *The Empowered Church* I make the statement "ministry builds people and leadership builds churches".

I have never personally had a goal of leading a large church. What I did many years ago was to make a personal goal to build bigger people. Once I realised the leadership versus ministry dichotomy, I had to develop ways to produce effective leaders. To this aim we have conducted training programmes, implemented an internship programme, encouraged attendance at seminars and the reading of leadership literature. But all of this was non-productive until we created a pathway for leadership development. The steps of this path-

---

17 In general this is true. However, sometimes really good strategic thinkers (level four) do not make good small group leaders or supervisors. As a result I have known churches which have successfully introduced people straight into level four!

way can be summarised as follows.

>> Identification of people with leadership potential

The 'L' factor has greatly aided me in this process of identification. However I, and others of my key leaders, have supplemented
the 'L' factor with the concept of 'leadership identification groups'.
These are special small groups involving both a person and their
spouse who we believe may have leadership potential. These groups
meet for anywhere between six to 12 months on a fortnightly basis. They involve the group in a case study exercise where I frame a
hypothetical situation and the group discusses how a leader might
respond.

In this context one can observe the presence of intellectual firepower, judgment, and the belief systems which exist within the people.

The group provides a form of training and the possibility of getting to know those in the groups better. Its greatest value, however, is
that of identification, not of development.

>> Involve potential leaders in a level one leadership task

I believe this is necessary in my organisation irrespective of
whether the person has held a level two, three or four level leadership role in another organisation either inside or outside the church.
More than anything else it is level one which will reveal the 'people
skills' of someone who might be bright, and may be able to deal with
significant complexity, but who would not be effective in an organisation like a church, made up principally of volunteers.

>> Recognise that each level has three phases

The three phases are that a person is:
a) learning to do the job;
b) doing the job; and
c) then ready to move on to a more complex task.

Not everyone will be able to move to c) and either may flounder at a) or be comfortable at b) and so not be ready to move on. The so called 'Peter Principle' recognises the fact that too often in organisations people who are competent at one level continue to be promoted until they reach a level of incompetence. Whilst this is always a risk it is better to recognise the three phases within a level such that, until they really are confident and show a capacity to move on, they are not promoted to phase a) of the next level of leadership.

>> A mentorship strategy

A mentorship programme should be in place such that the mentors are mentoring people two levels below the level at which they themselves function. This means that level one leaders should have access to mentoring by level three leaders, and level two leaders should have access to mentoring by level four leaders.

The reason for this approach is not always obvious. Let me go back to the concept of a cell leader and promoting assistant leaders when the leader moves on.

This concept works really well where the leader of a group at level one has been highly effective and has trained an assistant to take over. However, frequently the reason why people move out of a leadership role, at whatever level, is because they themselves are incapable of doing the task. Where this is the case it is unlikely that an ineffective leader would have been capable of training a competent replacement. Also they are often asked to suggest their replacement.

This clearly makes no sense and yet it is a process which is followed all too often. The leader who is choosing the replacement therefore needs to have access to two levels down in a mentoring capacity.

Although level two leaders do not report to level four, it is from level two that level three leaders will be appointed. And yet this is very difficult if the level four leaders have no contact with level two leaders. **It is therefore helpful to distinguish between task accountability and personal development**. Mentoring should not be limited by a person to those over which they exert accountability.

>> A process of personal development

As mentioned above it is important to distinguish between task accountability and personal development. As I have said, level threes report to levels fours but the mentoring of level threes is part of the responsibility of level five. In a good leadership development pathway the organisation will be structured so that level threes meet with level fours for the purposes of task accountability and definition but meet with their level five leader for the purposes of their ongoing personal development. This structure obviously breaks down between levels five and four because there is no level six. The explanation for this is that by the time a leader reaches level four leadership they have become proficient in terms of tasks required and mentoring others. Level five and four leaders frequently end up working together in teams, for example as a church executive.

In my experience it does not take long before level four leaders are at least as competent as the level five leaders in terms of tasks (in some cases more competent), but are still continuing to develop in what modern writers call emotional intelligence and in their spiritual and faith formations. This I suspect is more caught than taught in the interaction between the level five and four leaders. And the level five leader will gain ongoing mentoring through the peer relationships he or she establishes with others who are either in a similar role in another organisation, of the same kind, or an organisation of a completely different kind.

I have learned a lot from pastors of large churches who have gone where I am trying to go as a leader and I have also learned a lot from senior executives in large business organisations. They can't always help my emotional or spiritual development (though they may), but they have a lot to teach about the task of leading a large church, for they themselves are level five leaders in large organisations.

>> Identifying your leaders by levels

At my church we hold an annual leaders day each February to which leaders of every level are invited. At the time of writing, this is a group of close to 250 people. Of the 250 there is only one level five leader, four level four leaders, 20 or so level three leaders and the rest are either level two or level one. In identifying where all our leaders fit, in this model, we are able to visualise our pool of potential leaders and identify who needs development.

We are also able to identify the age of our leaders in the various levels. At 57 I am the only level five leader but I am not the oldest leader. Three of the four level four leaders are fifteen years or more my junior. This is really important because if all our level four leaders were also in their fifties, it is likely the group of us would be ready to retire gracefully at the same time without leaving the church proven and effective younger level four leaders.

Interestingly enough our oldest leaders are found at levels two and one. But since we are talking about a development pathway it's important that these older leaders do not stand in the way of the development of younger level one and two leaders who will be our potential future level four leaders.

I remember in my younger days as a chartered accountant with a major accounting firm, that the firm took the view that unless someone had been identified as a potential partner, then they were not allowed to continue as a manager in the firm much beyond the age of 35. There were a few exceptions to this rule because of people's specific technical skills, but they were normally moved sideways out of the leadership structure of the organisation so that young leaders could continue to develop in the firm. Frequently in the church the mistake has been made to allow level four and five leadership, particularly through board structures, to be dominated by people over the age of 50 thus frustrating young developing leaders.

>> Moving people sideways

I have already alluded to the fact that level three skills (systems capacity) are generic. This means that a good systems person would be capable leading in either a small group area, a discipleship area, a deacon's area and so on. If a young and effective level three leader is leading an area of ministry and is likely to be there for some time, it may be necessary to move someone from one ministry area to another to get level three experience. It is the role of the level four leader to explain that, for their own development, they need to be willing to move out of a ministry area to which they may be really committed.

>> Developing peer clusters

In the church there has been a tradition of putting people together on the basis of their ministry area or gifting. Obviously enormous benefits may be gained from this. However, once people move beyond level one greater benefit will be derived by putting people into clusters of people functioning at their level of leadership. Their roles will be similar even though the ministry areas they're involved in are different.

Level one and two leaders in a church are frequently volunteers, in full-time employment outside of the church (we do not begin to put people on staff until they have reached level three). We have found a programme of periodic breakfast meetings bringing people together who are fulfilling a similar leadership role to be very effective. Where there are only one or two people at say level three in a smaller church it is the responsibility of the level five leader to try and connect these people with similar leaders in other churches in their denomination or locality.

>> Annual assessments

Where leaders are on staff the concept of an annual assessment is appropriate to enable people to understand how they are going.

In some organisations the salary structure of the staff is related to level of leadership and at which phase of that level they are currently functioning. If someone has recently been promoted to level four and are in phase a), as discussed above, then they need to know whether they are still learning the role or whether they are now considered competent in the role. This would normally occur as part of an annual review which includes salary. They need to know whether, in the opinion of the person to whom they are accountable, they have moved beyond the learning stage and are now considered competent in the role. Because they understand that these three phases exist in each level then to be told they are still at level a) after only six months is not a negative assessment. By the time they get to level four they will know there is much learning required to function well at the new level to which they have been promoted.

However, with people at levels one, two and three an annual review is probably not enough. I would suggest a quarterly assessment be undertaken. However, this assessment should be very informal because these people are normally volunteers, not people on the payroll. Both the leader and the persons being assessed will benefit from the assessment. The leader will learn what additional support or training is required. And the person assessed will learn how their assessor perceives they are going. Just being listened to is very encouraging for volunteers.

Qualifications for Each Level of Development

I had initially intended to include the material which is set out immediately below as an appendix in this book. However, in a number of seminars that I have been running with Christian leaders over the last 18 months, questions have been asked about the qualifications necessary for each level of leadership. This has encouraged me to include these in the text of the chapter itself.

A leadership development pathway is not just a road with a series of gates. It is a process of intentionalised learning with acknowledgment that certain skills are being learned and mastered. Although such skill acquisition may be related to financial remuneration, as commonly occurs in the business world, it is also part of the learning process. Discouragement occurs when someone who has mastered certain skills is not acknowledged as having done so, and when someone who is promoted, without acquiring certain skills fails and often experiences discouragement which wouldn't have happened, had it been recognised that they were still developing the prerequisite skills for the new level of leadership.

In the qualifications set out below you will observe that, although it is primarily focussed at leadership development, there is provision for ministry skills as well. This is incorporated because particularly at levels four and three there is an important role in the church for people with ministry skills not just leadership skills. For example it is advisable for the church executive team, which is made up of level five and four people, to have someone with extensive pastoral experience. This is particularly so if the level five leader is not strong pastorally.

Apple Trees Produce Apples

At this point I also want to make another observation. We know that chickens produce chickens and apple trees produce apples, but what is not often acknowledged in organisations is that only leaders can reproduce leaders and pastors reproduce pastors. These are not capacities which can simply be taught by teachers. As a result people with certain ministry skills (eg, pastors) can be included in an executive board at level four, but ought not to be part of the leadership development pathway, unless they are also effective leaders. If someone is put into a level four leadership role on the basis of their ministry skills rather than proven leadership ability, not only will they be ineffective in that role but they will also be unable to reproduce leaders at levels two and three. In fact people with leadership ability will find it extremely frustrating being led by someone who is not a leader however gifted they may be in ministry.

Qualifications of Levels of Leadership

> Level Five
>> Qualifications
Able to competently develop, modify and implement systems for programmes of up to three years' duration.

Able to develop, modify and implement strategic plans from three to five years.

>> Roles

1. Mentor those doing one and two above.
2. Supervising two above.
3. View the organisation as a whole in five to 10 years.*

*Note: The person may:

- be a newcomer to this level (Phase (a));
- be competent but no longer growing (Phase (b)); or
- have mastered this level and still be developing (Phase (c)). This applies to all five levels.

> Level Four

>> Qualifications

1. Able to competently lead people in ministry.
2. Able to competently supervise people in leadership.
3. Able to competently develop, modify and implement systems for programmes of up to three years' duration or specific ministry or technical skills at a level above that possessed by level two and three people.

>> Roles

1. Mentor those doing two and three above.
2. Supervise three above.
3. Develop, modify and implement strategic plans for a period of three to five years; or specific ministry or technical skills at a level above that possessed by level two and three people.

> Level Three

>> Qualifications

1. Proven competency in an area of ministry.
2. Proven competent in leading an area of ministry or group.
3. Able to competently supervise people leading an area of ministry or group.

>> Roles

1. Mentor people doing two and three above.
2. Supervise two above
3. Develop, modify and implement systems for programmes of up to three year's duration; or pastor a group of at least 50 people.

> Level Two
>> Qualifications

1. Proven competence in an area of ministry.
2. Proven competent in leading an area of ministry or group.

>> Roles

1. Mentor people doing two above.
2. Supervise two above or pastor a group of at least 25 people.

> Level One
>> Qualifications

1. Proven commitment to the church's core values, purpose and general values.
2. Proven competency in an area of ministry.

>> Role

1. Lead an area of ministry or group.

Linking Pay Structures to Levels of Leadership

Within traditional denominations there are pay structures set by the denomination and these often assume:

1. that the church provides housing which helps neutralise cost of living variances from urban to rural environments and from one city to another;
2. that the paid members of staff, other than a church secretary or administrator, will normally be ordained clergy.

However, with the growth of larger churches a variety of different kinds of programme staff have begun to join the payroll. I have already mentioned people such as children's workers, youth workers or music directors and frequently, because of the nature of a leadership development pathway, these people will in time become pastoral staff.

I am constantly asked at the annual senior pastors' seminars I hold each year in Sydney, how the salaries for these ancillary staff should be set. For a number of years we used a concept whereby my salary, as the senior pastor, was used as the base salary and other staff received a percentage of my own. For example the assistant (associate) pastor received 80% of my salary, the church administrator received 75%, and new pastoral staff (ie, level three staff) received 60%.

This kind of salary structure seemed to work for a period of years and was borrowed from another organisation. However, it was unsatisfactory in that it failed to recognise the nature of leadership development and it did not reward the growing responsibility and complexity of tasks which people were dealing with. For this reason it was decided to link salaries to the five levels of leadership and the three phases within each level.

Set out below is a modified version of a recent salary structure developed by our church. Actual figures are not included as regional variances mean the actual salaries paid from region to region vary significantly.

Our church is situated in one of the most expensive areas in Sydney where rents are high and so the gross salary package has to take this into account. In addition, the church reimburses staff for certain ministry expenses which are not reflected in the schedule below. The purpose of including this information is to enable you to get a sense of how salaries progress in parallel to staff's growth through the leadership levels.

Table 7.1: Salary scales based on leadership levels

Position	Phases	Bench-Mark Low	Bench-Mark High
Level 5	a	90%	95%
	b	95%	100%
	c	100%	105%
Level 4	a	75%	80%
	b	80%	85%
	c	85%	90%
Level 3	a	60%	65%
	b	65%	70%
	c	70%	75%

Before moving on I want to make a couple of observations about the whole issue of salaries and leadership development.

Unless a pastor lacks any other skills and has had no previous work experience, then it is normally likely that a pastor would be able to earn more working for an organisation outside the church than for the church itself. This is another way of saying that people do not become involved in church life, and join the staff of churches, for financial reasons.

In saying this I am aware that things are changing. Because of Australian taxation legislation, through the provision of fringe benefits, clergy can no longer cry poor in the way that they used to. Be that as it may, very few clergy would say that they are paid what they're worth. They do not see themselves in the marketplace trying to gain maximum financial benefit for the provision of their services. However, increasing someone's financial remuneration, within the above scales, is a way of recognising that they are developing as a leader, that the responsibilities that they have to deal with are increasing, and such factors are recognised by those responsible for setting their wage levels.

Also annual adjustments, based on the Consumer Price Index, are needed to take into account the impact of inflation, so that an adequate standard of living is preserved for the staff and their families.

Teams at Levels

As organisations like churches grow it is normally advisable to create teams of leaders at each level above level one. These teams are then able to engage in 'strategic conversations' both at their own levels and with those in other levels. The tools presented next may be used by individuals or by teams participating in such 'strategic conversations'.

CHAPTER EIGHT

VISIONING CAPACITY

Pastor Steven Slough sat back in his chair in the study, at the back of the church, and pondered over the problem of the fact that although the church was full, a reflection of the health of the church, the budget was fully spent and they needed more space. According to the books he'd read on the subject he probably had two alternatives: enlarge the size of the church sanctuary or add a fifth service to the already busy Sunday schedule.

Because of commitments to small groups a mid-week service was not an option and there was already a service on Saturday afternoons for couples with young families.

Steven had contacted the church growth consultant at his denomination to discuss the problem and was presented with the normal alternatives. He'd rung three or four other churches in his denomination, which he knew had faced a similar situation, and was again presented with the two options.

And yet there was something within Steven which was saying to him that neither of these alternatives was the way for his church to go at this stage of its development. Many years before they had attempted a church plant by sending a group of people from the congregation, but for a number of reasons this had not been successful and he wasn't inclined to go down this pathway again.

They were already having difficulties with neighbours due to the number of cars parking in the streets around the church on Sunday, and they had also received a letter of complaint related to the noise generated as the band rehearsed for Sunday services.

Steven had never shirked a challenge and yet sensed that another service would over-tax his own personal capacity to stay fresh during the day and would also put increased pressure on the music ministry of the church which was already functioning at capacity.

Logic told him that the advice he had been given was sound but he sensed that to take either option would not be good for the church.

Instead of calling in his associate pastor, which is what he would normally do, on the spur of the moment he called in his creative director. When Helen walked into his office he knew that she would not have the answer he was looking for, but he was hoping that she might help him to think about the problem a different way. The conversation, which followed, went something like this:

Steven: Helen, I have a problem which does not seem to have a logical answer. You know me well enough to know that I normally problem solve by adding up all the factors, analysing, and then coming to a logical conclusion. I've done all this I don't like the answer which logic wants to present to me. You creative types seem to approach problem solving differently. Just how do you do it?

Helen: Well, when I problem solve I start with mind mapping. I respect my cognitive capacities but I know there are times when there is no right answer and I want to intuitively engage the problem to think through all the options. Three years ago you sent me to a seminar about thinking tools to improve my skills as a leader, and I've been using a couple of them ever since.

Steven: I think you've just nicely said to me that perhaps I should have gone to the course instead of you.

Helen: Well the first thing I found interesting about the seminar was that the fellow who was the presenter is a consultant to government and big business about leadership matters, but hasn't done a single course on business. In fact his background was not business at all, he was the head of the English literature department of a major high school. For years he spent his time teaching high school students how to think creatively and then one day, almost by accident, he discovered that the creative processes he was teaching his students could apply equally to the work environment where people who were leaders were required to be creative and not just logical in problem solving.

Steven: Are you telling me that you don't have to be creative to be intuitive? That it's not just musicians or artists or poets who are able to be creative?

Helen: That's exactly what I am saying. Let me tell you about one of the tools which I was taught called mind mapping…

What the Leadership Pathway won't Accomplish

The leadership pathway provides a context in which people can develop the skills which are necessary to become effective leaders in the context of the church. Not everyone can walk all the way through the pathway as the increasing complexity will set ceilings as to how far they can go before they become ineffective.

Part of the process of developing someone with leadership potential is the acquisition of thinking skills. As I've stated earlier, the 'L' factor, identifies the need for intellectual firepower and good judgment in leaders. Though these faculties are given (ie, we are born with them) they are capable of significant development. Traditionally in a western education, children were taught not just what they need to know but also how to think. In classical times the study of rhetoric was part of one's high school education and Greek writers like Aristotle were mandatory reading in the development of people of influence.

There came a point of time in western education where it was decided that the purpose of education was not to teach people how to think, but rather to teach them what the educators believed they needed to know. When I went to school I was encouraged to do languages, particularly Latin, because my father considered that language learning would improve my capacity for logic. At the time I doubted the value of the process, but he may have been right. One thing I'm sure of however, is that studying Latin did nothing for developing my intuitive side or mycapacity for creative problem solving. Doing degrees in both accounting and theology were both dependent on my capacity to think logically and memorise and neither required any great capacity for creativity or intuition. As a result, by the age of 35, I was confident logically but inept creatively.

Then I met my friend Tony Golsby-Smith, the high school teacher in the story above. The two thinking tools I am going to describe below are Tony's inventions. Because he is in my debt, due to my introducing him to the wonderful game of golf, he has generously given permission for me to incorporate these tools in this particular book.

Mind Mapping

Mind mapping, through the use of spider diagrams, is a technique designed to access what we intuitively (unconsciously) think. The process in no way negates or rejects the power of reason and the application of logic.

However, long ago it was Aristotle, the tutor of Alexander the Great, who observed that not every question has a right answer! Aristotle states that some problems have a right answer (eg, 1 + 1 = 2). But in many cases the answer is 'good' rather than 'right'. He assumes there is not enough information available to be able to determine a 'right' answer. There may be too many unknowns, or the situation is changing so quickly that yesterdays 'facts' are no longer relevant.

Where this is the case the leader will need to decide intuitively rather than logically. We often describe this as a 'gut feeling' to distinguish it from a mental process.

To learn how to access our intuitive capacity when we need it we need to have tools which will temporarily deactivate our cognitive faculties.

Spider diagramming is one such method. It is helpful to see a map so I include the following which I did when considering what to do with a service which was struggling to grow in numbers.

When doing a spider diagram (map) there are a few common problems (syndromes) Tony has detected when people are learning the skill. These problems are discussed briefly after the principles are outlined.

8.1 The Process

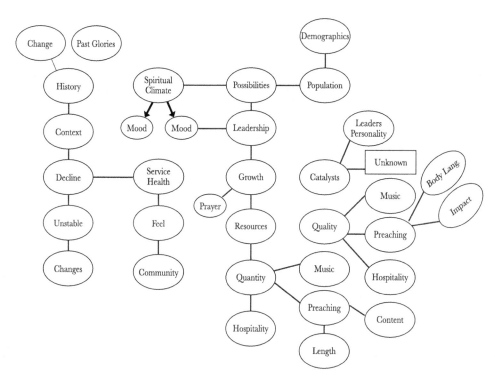

1. The first circle on the page contains the issue we are wanting to consider in this case.

2. A noun or adjective is permissible but no clauses or phrases. Once these are used our cognitive mental processes cut in and the intuitive side of the brain disengages.

3. Lists are to be avoided (eg, a list of feelings) because again the process becomes cognitive.

4. The sequence of creating the chain of ideas is not important. In the above spider diagram, the linkages are what is important. *Note*, 'service health' was linked to 'decline', and 'feel'. 'Decline' was linked to 'unstable' and 'changes'. 'Growth' was linked to 'leadership', 'resources', 'prayer' and 'catalysts'. 'Catalysts' was linked to 'leaders', 'personality' and 'unknown'. From the central topic 'service health' random thoughts emerge.

5. During the process the words should 'pop out', and not be the result of time spent 'thinking'. They need to be spontaneous. If following one thread you exhaust the spontaneous words go back to a word and begin a new thread of thought.

6. Good maps are messy because you are in a process of discovery.

7. Maps are spatial not linear — they exist in two dimensions.

8. The lines are vital. They indicate the relationships between ideas.

9. The edge of the page is the boundary of your thought so use an A2 or A1 sized page.

10. Don't put too many words inside a bubble — just enough to 'hook' the idea.

11. Start in the middle and sprawl outwards.

The following dangers exist:

    1.   *The Daisy Chain Syndrome*

Although you've cut down on words, this is just a 'list' with bubbles. It indicates 'one track' thinking. Remember maps are spatial not linear.

2.   *The One Ring Syndrome*

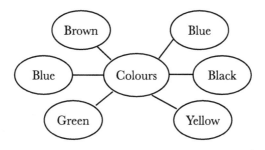

You've run short of imaginative gas. Perhaps you're cautious and won't let go. The richness emerges at the edges, away from the centre. Close your eyes and try to see one of your bubbles. Doodle with the map. Then go out further.

3.   *Wordy Syndrome*
This means that there are too many words in a bubble, which end up diminishing the visual feedback. Look for key words. Go over each bubble and highlight one key word as a 'hook'. Then try again on a new subject.

4.   *No bubbles Syndrome*

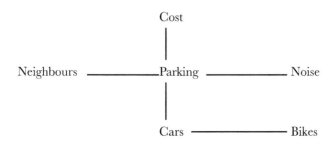

This is only half-way better than a list. The feedback is too verbal, and without structure — like a 'dog's breakfast'. In this syndrome there is very little structure and shape. Draw bubbles and try a map without words — just bubbles and symbols.

The use of spider mapping is a wonderful tool for leaders when thinking about the future and the issues which must be addressed for vision fulfilment.

As a technique, mind mapping through the use of spider diagrams, is also an excellent tool when preparing to write reports or research papers. It can provide the skeleton from which writing can occur and help determine what further research needs to be undertaken.[18]

The ABCD™ model

This next tool, also the invention of Dr Golsby-Smith, relates to the process of deciding what action may need to be taken by an organisation. Let me begin by simply explaining what each letter stands for.

A 'What's going on?'— a clear understanding of the present situation.

B 'But what are our aspirations?' What do we want to see happen in the future?

C 'So what might we do?'

D 'Now how do we make it happen?'

In the model it is pointed out how frequently leaders and leadership teams go from A (what's going on?) to C (what might we do?) and then on to D (how do we make it happen?), before considering B (what do we want to see happen in the future?).

The model also embraces the concept of a 'thinking wave', as depicted below.

The thinking wave starts at A (what's going on?) and explores further to the point where C (a hypothesis) develops. However, often just

---

18 The suggestions, but not the map, come from the manual *Thinking with Pictures*, copyrighted by Golsby-Smith & Associates and are included by permission.

when C (what we might do?) is forming and we are about to consider D (how we might make it happen?), we realise we are no longer confident we are sure what is actually going on at present (A) so we go back to A for further thought.

Consider the following diagram:

Diagram 8.2: ABCD model

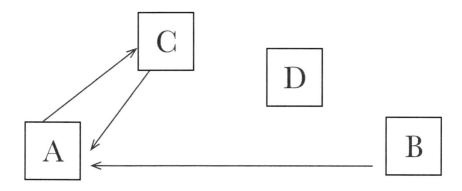

Remember Pastor Slough at the beginning of this chapter? In his own mind he travelled from A to C. Then he sought advice and again travelled from A to C but was still unsure what to do. He then used a spider diagram to rethink A again. As he did so he realised that a bigger sanctuary or another service were not the only options. The composition of the church had changed over the past two years and there were a large number of youth and children in the service. He was surprised when both these words were in bubbles attached to demographics and yet neither his friends nor the consultant had focussed on their presence in the service. There were always between 80 to 100 youth in the main service in the morning and almost twice that number of children.

He sat back and considered the impact of almost 300 seats being available for growth and called a meeting with the youth and children's pastors. There were still problems to be solved. But he had seen the A (what's going on?) differently and realised the B (what we want to see happen in the future) they were working toward had never had input from the children's and youth perspective. He now had a new C (what might we do?) floating around in his head but D (how we might make it happen?) was definitely a decision for others.

Because of the nature of the thinking wave, when the meeting was held, the discussions bounced back and forwards between A and C before a C was finally agreed upon. The three pastors shared an agreed B (a common vision of the future) and now began to recruit others to develop a strategic plan to see this vision fulfilled.

Strategic Planning (D)

So often D is neglected or handled poorly. Often those involved in D (how we might make it happen) have not taken part in the thinking wave discussions and are poorly briefed on A and B. They are presented with C (what might we do?) and told to work out a D without understanding the needs for the changes and what they are really trying to achieve.

Good books on strategic planning[19] are helpful but deal only with D- type issues. This is why simple thinking tools, like those presented above, can help avoid the enormous waste of people's time in planning strategies which don't solve the real problems facing a church or ministry.

Outcome

Pastor Slough called a joint meeting of the leaders of the youth and children's ministry of the church. He lead them in a strategic conversation of the overcrowding problem using the ABCD model. It quickly emerged that both leaders (of children and youth) had unspoken aspirations (B'S) that would involve special children's and youth services running simultaneously with the adult service. However, many parents wanted their families to worship together, if only

19   Eg, Malphurs, A. *Advanced Strategic Planning*. Baker Books, 1999.

for part of the service. A six month trial period was undertaken at the end of which parents pleaded that their children **not** be brought back into the service. Their children and youth were having a great time and it was obvious to everyone that the church was growing again.

CHAPTER NINE

SKILFUL HANDS

The Empowered Church dealt with the issue of leadership (skilful hands) rather than with the identifying and development of leaders. Consequently quadrant four on the book cover was dealt with first because of my desire to communicate the difference and confusion which exists between leadership and ministry.

Since writing that book I have become familiar with some excellent new ideas on 'change management', and so at the end of this book I felt I should include this material rather than keep it for a third volume.

I am also aware that adopting a 'levels of leadership' approach to leadership development will mean that most churches may have to introduce significant change. Contrary to popular belief many people in churches are not against change. But they are certainly opposed to change introduced poorly and change which is perceived to be unjust.

'Mythologies' develop as groups of members attribute motives to those who have initiated change. A culture forms within a church when people share assumptions about whether change reflects positive or negative values.

Effective leaders are aware that cultures form and set out to proactively create the culture of the church. The difficulty is that there are frequently levels of leaders between key decision makers and those most affected by the decisions, as illustrated below.

Diagram 9.1: Levels of leaders

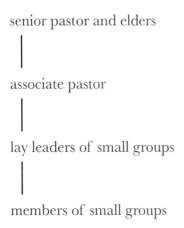

senior pastor and elders

associate pastor

lay leaders of small groups

members of small groups

If the elders of a church decide to change the focus of small groups from Bible studies to outreach there are two levels of leaders between those affected and the decision makers.

The small group members will try and determine the 'motives' behind the 'actions' and the resulting beliefs, if shared by the whole group, become a myth potentially causing a culture resistant to future change.

The leader's behaviour must be totally consistent with his or her stated values. Members of the small groups are often unable to be present to listen to the discussion as to why the change should be made, so the leader's behaviour becomes the symbol underlying the myth.

Members of churches can handle many small changes provided the process of change does not clash with the prevailing values of the church. It is the change of systems (eg, the way small groups function) which have the greatest impact. Such changes are interpreted as demonstrating how the church values its members.

Nature of Systems

Not all systems are the same. Studies have found that systems can be categorised into two types:

1. **Systems that differentiate**: The most obvious forms of this type of system are titles and pay scales for staff and volunteers.
2. **Systems that equalise**: An example of this would be the fact that the pastor does not have his own special parking space but parks where everyone else does. Or the fact that everyone lines up for morning tea irrespective of their title.

The changes which have to be most carefully implemented are those which shift a system from one type to another.

Pastor Bill Sheepgate and his associate Graeme Speed are discussing the introduction of a new pastoral care system for the church. Previously the church had relied on its small groups as the basic providers of care. However, there was a strong desire to see the groups focus more on outreach. A team of lay people had been chosen and trained in pastoral care. The new system was soon to be launched and the question of titles to be used for this new team of people was being discussed.

Ps Bill: Graeme, what are you going to call these new carers? What title are you going to give them?

Ps Graeme: Well we've thought quite a lot about that. We don't want to call them 'pastoral carers' because that term contains baggage we are trying to avoid. We previously had a system with 'pastoral carers' which didn't work. We are considering the terms 'pastor' or 'lay pastor'.

Ps Bill: I see problems with both suggestions. The term 'pastor' differentiates leaders who are on staff and are being paid by the church from the leaders who are volunteers. I think the pastoral team might be upset if they lose one of the few distinctions which reflects the monetary sacrifice they are making to work for the church.

I also see a problem with the term 'lay pastor'. We have always avoided the use of the phrase 'lay ministry' as it often seems to undervalue or demean the work done by sincere members of the church.

Ps Graeme: Well we have to call them something and the team chosen will be a powerful symbol of how highly or lowly the leadership of the church views their role.

Ps Bill: Why not use the term 'pastoral assistant'? It maintains the recognition given staff pastors and avoids the lay/clergy dichotomy.

How Systems are Viewed and Changed

A leader can achieve significant change if he or she can discern systems that are unfair, dishonest or show a significant lack of trust. Such systems, over time, develop a mythology that is negative.

The role of the leader is to change the negative culture by shifting the system either:
- from equalisation to differentiation; or
- from differentiation to equalisation.

For example, a church has had a long tradition of hymns in the 10 am service. Half the members love the hymns and want nothing to change, though they are a declining minority. The majority is split into two groups. One wants to scrap hymns to switch entirely to contemporary music. The other will settle for a mix of the old and the new.

The 'oldies' know that the evening service already has contemporary music and feel that to change 'their' service would be unfair because it differentiates the morning from the evening.

The two groups who want change are not considering the evening service but rather the growing church, of the same denomination, which is only a few kilometres away. They have noticed young families are beginning to drift to that church and want to move from differentiation to equalisation.

The group who wants to have both hymns and contemporary music don't realise that they want to have both kinds of system changes at the same time. The result is likely to be that those with negative views of the present music (system) will increase as there will now be three myths, two of which are negative.

How Change is Viewed[20]

Researchers have concluded that to achieve change which alters the status of a system, as described above, the leader needs to understand how such a change will be evaluated. This assumes there are a basic set of values which all people share and which are part of the cohesion of a group of people who regularly meet. These basic values are considered to be:

- trust;
- love;
- dignity;
- courage;
- fairness; and
- honesty.

In groups, behaviour will be assessed on a continuum depicted as follows.

---

20 This section is highly influenced by Macdonald, H, Macdonald R, and Stewart, K. 'Leadership: A New Direction', *British Army Review* 93, 1989.

Table 9.1: Positive and negative change assessment

Positive	*Negative*
trustworthy	untrustworthy
loving	unloving
respectful of human dignity	lack of respect of human dignity
fair	unfair
courageous	cowardly
honest	dishonest

I will illustrate these values with two examples. The first is a grossly exaggerated example of the negative.

> Negative

Pastor Greg Sly meets with a group of elderly members of the 10 am service. He assures them he respects the fact that they have belonged to the church for decades and that the now deceased husbands of some of them had built the present church when the old one burnt down. He assures them that he really cares for them and respects their right to have the church remain as it has always been.

Three months later the first contemporary song is introduced during communion, accompanied only by an acoustic guitar. Over the next 18 months a band is gradually formed and as musicians are added the noise level gradually increases to the point where the older members are experiencing earaches and there is now only one hymn, played by the organ, while the offering is being taken.

Church members increase so much that one Sunday Pastor Sly announces that a new 8.00 am traditional service will begin in a few weeks. The old members meet to discuss this new proposal. They think it is unfair (they have not been consulted); it is a cowardly act (Pastor Sly would not discuss it) and it is dishonest because it is contrary to what Pastor Sly had said to them when they had met previously.

They decide as a group they will stay together but move to another small church nearby. One by one (after conversation over tea) they call their solicitors and alter their wills!

Now lets consider the example using positive values.

> Positive

Pastor Greg Sly meets with a group of elderly members of the 10 am service. He assures them he respects the fact that they have belonged to the church for decades and that he knows that the dead husbands of some of them had built the church when the old one burnt down. He assures them he really cares for them and respects their right to have the church remain as it has always been.

Three months later he asks to meet with the elderly group again. He tells them that trust in leadership has always been a hallmark of the church and he doesn't want to do anything which will damage the church now, or the trust which future leaders will enjoy. He tells them of the steady decline in both attendance and finances such that the denomination is no longer willing to subsidise his salary.

He states that they have every right to expect the church to continue to care for them and he is committed personally to showing God's love to each one of them.

He states that he respects them, and their opinion, and needs their help. Can they help him so that the church they love does not close, but continues as a memorial to their many friends and family members who are no longer here?

Mary Brownlow, the widow of a previous presiding elder, speaks first. The others always respect what she says and listen carefully. Mary says, "This is my church and I don't want to lose it or leave it. But I am very unhappy that my children and grandchildren now go to the church in the next suburb. I might be willing to change just don't ask me to put up with the awful loud music the youth have in the evening".

Pastor Sly respects her honesty and speaks slowly knowing there is a lot at risk. He begins by asking a question: "Am I right in saying that these days most or all of you wake early and fill in time waiting for the 10 am service?" Their heads nod in unison as they recall how important 10 am was when they needed time to get the kids ready, and even then it seemed a rush.

He goes on, "If we held an 8.00 am service would you, as a group, become pioneers again to help me start the service? The music will be what you love and respect, only the organ will play, and there could be a special morning tea in the rectory garden or inside if it is cold". He then adds, "Honestly, I think it is best for the church and for you but to change without your consent and active involvement would be dishonest. You know some ministers are afraid of the older members and try and change things gradually. What I am suggesting will require courage by you and me but I don't think you want a cowardly minister".

He leaves them alone and comes back 20 minutes later.

Again Mary speaks for the group: "We are sad at what is happening to the church and will miss going to the 10 am service. However, you have treated us with dignity, have been honest and fair. As a group we will support you and tell those who couldn't be here that we think it will be a positive change for the church and also for us".

After a few months Mary speaks to the group again. She suggests that after church during the gap before lunch they could meet at various homes to make things for their grandchildren. Most agree, and the groups begin meeting at people's houses after church. At one of these gatherings Mary drops the fact that she has recently altered her will to add a bequest to the church. She notices the group is growing as others begin to join their church from that noisy church nearby.

Difference between Change and Transition

There seems to be considerable confusion between change and transition. **Change** is the new situation we are trying to create (a new culture, a new system etc). **Transition** is the psychological process people will have to go through to reach or create that new situation.

If you want to change jobs then the change is the nature of the new job. The transition starts long before the change and continues long after you have begun the new job.

The change may appear to have been achieved successfully but the transition is critical. If people do not complete the transition, the change doesn't last.

Distinctions between change and transition include:
- transition is an experience, change is an event;
- transition is psychological, change is situational;
- transition is process focused, change is outcome focused; and
- transition is always gradual and slow, change is relatively quick.

Because changes are occurring so quickly within the church both clergy and people are having difficulty transitioning psychologically, emotionally and spiritually.

Change does last if an effective transition is achieved.

Pastor Ann Smith had completed five years as the assistant pastor of a church in a medium sized city in southern Australia. Without warning she received a 'call' to become the pastor of a struggling church in the capital city of her state. After prayer and consulting friends and a denominational leader, she accepted the call. Ann packed all her earthly possessions into her VW and the attached trailer and headed for the 'big smoke'.

She moved into the house with her dog Ozzie and her parrot Ted. There were lots of bookshelves for her books and the house, though old, was comfortable and had been well maintained.

Twelve months later she seemed to others to have accomplished the change with minimal fuss. Internally the situation was completely different. She had not yet completed her transition. And she would not until the future of a friendship, which had begun in the previous church, was resolved as to its outcome.

Little did the leaders of the new church know how close she was to leaving the ministry to go back and marry the man she loved.

Greensville Church of Christ had hired church consultants to advise and implement change with a view to rectifying the declining health of the church's finances.

Although church membership and attendance had remained static for the last five years, the church's income had declined on average four per cent each year and with rising costs it was struggling to maintain its staff and facilities.

The consultants 'Dollars and Incense' recommended that the church abandon a weekly envelope system which had been introduced in the 1950s. In its place would be a programme utilising modern technologies such as bank to bank transfers, Eftpos, and computer based tithing.

The chairman of the elders, didn't own a computer and didn't know how to use an ATM machine. He was impressed by the growth figures being projected but wondered who would maintain the new system when the consultants left.

The launch Sunday seemed to go well but three months later the 60 year old church secretary resigned due to stress. When the church treasurer went through her desk he found her bottom two drawers filled with forms completed by members but never entered in the new computer system and others requiring forwarding to the church's bank.

It was no surprise that income had dropped a further 20 per cent in only three months. Change had occurred but not transition.

Impact of the Failure to Transition

When you make a change in your church, you put people into transition. If people cannot get through the transition, then the change will not work. It is so easy to preach change without offering assistance or support during the transition period.

> Three Phases of Transition
>> *One — an ending*
The person or people must let go of church life the way it was.
>> *Two — neutral zone*
This is the psychological state where people have left the past behind but have not emotionally embraced the new concept.
>> *Three — new beginning*
This happens when the new concept has psychologically been embraced, behaviour has changed to accept the new concept and when people are conscious that life is permanently moving in a new direction.

In reality during change these three phases overlap so it is possible to be in all three phases at the same time.

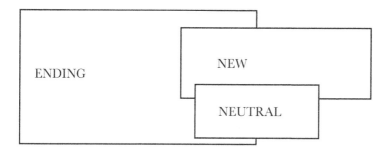

The failure to recognise that different people will move through these phases at different speeds creates the marathon effect. The senior pastor may be so far ahead of the people in the church it seems he is running in a different race.

Although the leader talks about where the church or ministry area is going, others are way behind him struggling to keep up with his latest new plan or strategy.

The leader is talking about change but the team is still processing the last transition. If time is not allowed for a proper transition then behaviour may change temporarily but beliefs won't change. It seems like everything is changed but nothing is different.

People resist transition not change. They may intellectually recognise that a change is good for the church, but they have to emotionally negotiate each of the three phases and frequently quit doing the neutral phase. There is resistance to letting go of the old ways, to being nowhere, and to trying something new.

Leaders often focus on where the team ought to be in the process of change instead of understanding where the team members actually are in the transition.

Are they struggling to let go of the old? What can you do to help them to be secure until they embrace the new concept? Are they in limbo?

Sometimes when churches change pastors, particularly after a lengthy pastorate, a new pastor is appointed too soon before the church has been through the first two phases of transition. They are still in love with their old pastor and are not yet able to lovingly embrace the new pastor. For this reason some churches will find a three to nine month interim pastor as a helpful strategy.

In the neutral zone there are a number of things you can do.

1. Positive talk is important but doesn't always speed up the process.
2. In transition the old world has to die. This is difficult as it is often a place where people lived and loved.
3. Use the neutral time creatively to begin to imagine the possibilities created by the changes ahead. It is a time of searching where you don't know how things will turn out.

Many churches endure cycles of growth, decline and renewal. This process can be helped by change agents who understand the nature and needs of transition.[21][22]

---

21 This discussion about the distinction between change and transition is influenced by Bridges, W. *Managing Transition, Making the Most of Change*, Perseus Books.

22 I highly recommend that this chapter be read in conjunction with section three of my book *Re-engineering the Church* mentioned at the back of this book.

CHAPTER TEN

CONCLUSION

Whether we like it or not the senior leaders of churches and other Christian organisations have a huge responsibility. A responsibility which requires them one day to give an account to the true head of the church (Heb 13:17). In some ways it is like comparing the role of parents to that of a baby sitter.

For many years Christian leaders were like baby sitters. All that was required of them was that when the job was over the kids were alive and well and had been kept safe.

Nowadays the role of the Christian leader is much more like that of the parent. They have the responsibility of providing a safe home (a place of love, nurture and feeding). But also they must lead the children through various stages of personal growth while the world outside the home is also changing rapidly. The parents both provide stability and initiate change where it is necessary.

The central thesis of this book has been that leaders are 'born' but can also be 'made' into more effective leaders. For this to happen at least three things are really helpful.

1. We need to identify people with leadership potential early. Either when they are young or when they are young Christians.

2. We need to provide a pathway they can take to make that development possible.

3. We need to never forget that each potential leader is a human

being with feelings, ideas and beliefs not just abilities.

Alistair Mant, quoted earlier in the book, has a saying I really like. He says "An organisation is a frog not a bicycle". By this he means that you can interchange the wheels from different bikes and they still work. You can do the same with the seats and the headlamps. But you can't swap the head of one frog with another nor can you put a head where the leg should be. Frogs are living things unlike bikes.

Christian organisations are made up of people not just names and positions. We need to be very careful how we implement processes designed to help people grow and make them more effective.

Organisations are Frogs not Bicycles

In the Preface to this book I referred the reader to Philippians 2:22 for reflection. As I finish this work I want to return to this verse. It has reminded me that the discipleship of leaders:

1. Can be observed as to its effect. Paul says "you know that Timothy has proved himself". Because of this I challenge you to examine honestly the fruit of your present discipleship and development programmes. If people are growing in maturity in Christ that is wonderful. If people are discovering and using their ministry gifts, that is very encouraging. But the question is, "Is there evidence you are discipling Godly effective leaders?"

2. It is not just about ability but also character. The word 'proved' in the NIV is the Greek word 'dokimen'. It occurs seven times in six verses of the New Testament (Rom 5:4; 2 Cor 2:9; 8:2; 9:13; 13:3 and Phil 2:22). In Romans it is translated as 'character'. In 2 Cor 2:9 and 8:2 it refers to testing and trial. In 2 Cor 9:13 it is again translated as 'proved', and in 13:3 'proof'. Thus we can deduce that the process of discipling leaders involves a context in which the character of a person is proved by trial and testing.

3. Occurs in a relational context in which a servant heart is required. Timothy served Paul in the work of the gospel.

May the Lord protect his church from gifted leaders who do not have servant hearts.

SUGGESTED READING

The 'L' Factor

Gardner, H. *Leading Minds*. Harper Collins, 1997.
Mant, A. *Intelligent Leadership*. Allen & Unwin, 1997.

Emotional Intelligence (EQ)

Goleman, D. *Emotional Intelligence*. Bloomsbury, 1996.
Goleman, D. *Working with Emotional Intelligence*. Bloomsbury, 1998.

Strategic Planning

Malphurs, A. *Advanced Strategic Planning*. Baker Books, 1999.

BASIS FOR KEY STAFF AND LEADERSHIP EVALUATION

Name: _____

Average Scores
(Code: 5 is high, 1 is low. Please circle score)

1. **Self Perception**
(a) **Emotional Awareness** (2 Cor 4:7–12)

    1   2   3   4   5

Recognising one's emotions and their effects.
People with this competence:
• *Know which emotions they are feeling and why.*
• *Realise the links between their feelings and what they think, do and say.*
• *Recognise how their feelings affect their performance.*
• *Have a guiding awareness of their values and goals.*

(b) **Accurate Self-Assessment** (Rom 12:3–8)

    1   2   3   4   5

Knowing one's inner resources, abilities, and limits.
People with this competence are:

- *Aware of their strengths and weaknesses.*
- *Reflective, learning from experience.*
- *Open to candid feedback, new perspectives, continuous learning, and self-development.*
- *Able to show a sense of humour and perspective about themselves.*

a) **Self-Confidence** (2 Tim 1:11–12)

1   2   3   4   5

A strong sense of one's self-worth and capabilities.

People with this competence:

- *Present themselves with self-assurance — have "presence".*
- *Can voice views that are unpopular and go out on a limb for what is right.*
- *Are decisive, able to make sound decisions despite uncertainties and pressures.*

2. Self-Government

a) **Self-Control** (2 Tim 1:7)

1   2   3   4   5

Keeping disruptive emotions and impulses in check.

People with this competence:

- *Manage their impulsive feelings and distressing emotions well.*
- *Stay composed, positive, and unflappable even in trying moments.*
- *Think clearly and stay focused under pressure.*

b) **Trustworthiness** (2 Thess 3:7–10)

1   2   3   4   5

Maintaining integrity.

People with this competence

- *Act ethically and are above reproach.*

- *Build trust through their reliability and authenticity.*
- *Admit their own mistakes and confront unethical actions in others.*
- *Take tough, principled stands even if they are unpopular.*

c) **Conscientiousness** (2 Cor 1:18–20)

1   2   3   4   5

Taking responsibility for personal performance.

People with this competence:

- *Meet commitments and keep promises.*
- *Hold themselves accountable for meeting their objectives.*
- *Are organised and careful in their work.*

d) **Adaptability** (Mark 1:32–38)

1   2   3   4   5

Being flexible in responding to change.

People with this competence:

- *Smoothly handle multiple demands, shifting priorities, and rapid change.*
- *Adapt their responses and tactics to fit fluid circumstances.*
- *Are flexible.*

e) **Innovation** (1 Cor 9:19–23)

1   2   3   4   5

Being open to novel ideas and approaches.

People with this competence:

- *Seek out fresh ideas from a wide variety of sources.*
- *Entertain original solutions to problems.*
- *Generate new ideas.*
- *Take fresh perspectives and risks in their thinking.*

3. Purpose Led

a) **Achievement Drive** (1 Cor 9:24–27)

1   2   3   4   5

Striving to improve or meet a standard of excellence.

People with this competence:

- *Are result-oriented, with a high drive to meet their objectives and standards.*
- *Set challenging goals and take calculated risks.*
- *Pursue information to reduce uncertainty and find ways to do better.*
- *Learn how to improve their performance.*

b) **Commitment** (Phil 1:27; 2:1–4)

1   2   3   4   5

Aligning with the goals of a group or organisation.

People with this competence:

- *Readily make sacrifices to meet larger organisational goals.*
- *Find a sense of purpose in the larger mission.*
- *Use the group's core values in making decisions and clarifying choices.*
- *Actively seeks out opportunities to fulfil the group's mission.*

c) **Initiative** (Col 4:5–6)

1   2   3   4   5

Displaying proactivity.

People with this competence:

- *Are ready to seize opportunities.*
- *Pursue goals beyond what's required or expected of them.*
- *Cut through red tape and bend the rules when necessary to get the job done.*
- *Mobilise others through unusual, enterprising efforts.*

d) **Optimism** (Heb 12:2–3)

1   2   3   4   5

Persistence.

People with this competence:

• *Persist in seeking goals despite obstacles and setbacks.*

• *Operate from hope of success rather than fear of failure.*

• *See setbacks as due to manageable circumstances rather than a personal flow.*

4. People Focus

a) **Understanding Others** (Jas 1:19)

1   2   3   4   5

Sensing others' feelings and perspectives, and taking an active interest in their concerns.

People with this competence:

• *Are attentive to emotional cues and listen well.*

• *Show sensitivity and understand others' perspectives.*

• *Help out based on an understanding other people's needs and feelings.*

b) **Developing Others** (Eph 4:11–12)

1   2   3   4   5

Sensing others' development needs and bolstering their abilities.

People with this competence:

• *Acknowledge and reward people's strengths and accomplishments.*

• *Offer useful feedback and identify people's needs for further growth.*

• *Mentor, give timely coaching, and offer assignments that challenge and foster a person's skills.*

c) **Ministry Sensitive** (Gal 5:13)

1   2   3   4   5

Anticipating, recognising, and meeting visitors and members needs.

People with this competence:

- *Understand members' needs and match them to ministries provided.*
- *Seek ways to increase members' satisfaction and loyalty.*
- *Gladly offer appropriate assistance.*
- *Grasp a member's perspective.*

d) Synergy Sensitive (1 Cor 1:26–29)

1   2   3   4   5

Cultivating opportunities through different kinds of people.

People with this competence:

- *Respect and relate well to people from varied backgrounds.*
- *Understand diverse worldviews and are sensitive to group differences.*
- *See diversity as opportunity, creating an environment where diverse people can thrive.*
- *Challenge bias and intolerance.*

e) Power Awareness (1 Kgs 12:25–28)

1   2   3   4   5

Understanding personal and position power.

People with this competence:

- *Accurately read key power relationships.*
- *Detect crucial social networks.*
- *Understand the forces that shape views and actions of members and visitors.*
- *Accurately read organisational and external realities.*

4. Influence

a) Communication (1 Cor 4:14–15)

1   2   3   4   5

Listening openly and sending messages.

People with this competence:

- *Are effective in give-and-take, registering emotional cues in attuning their message.*
- *Deal with difficult issues straightforwardly.*
- *Listen well, seek mutual understanding, and welcome sharing of information fully.*
- *Foster open communication and stay receptive to bad news as well as good.*

b) Conflict Management (Gal 6:15)

1   2   3   4   5

Negotiating and resolving disagreements.

People with this competence:

- *Handle difficult people and tense situations with diplomacy and tact.*
- *Spot potential conflict, bring disagreements into the open, and help de-escalate situations.*
- *Encourage debate and open discussion.*
- *Orchestrate win–win solutions.*

c) Leadership (Phil 2:19–24)

1   2   3   4   5

Inspiring and guiding individuals and groups.

People with this competence:

- *Articulate and arouse enthusiasm for a shared vision and mission.*
- *Step forward to lead as needed, regardless of position.*
- *Guide the performance of others while holding them accountable.*

- *Lead by example.*

d) **Change and Transition Management** (Gal 2:6–14)

1   2   3   4   5

Initiating or managing change.

People with this competence:

- *Recognise the need for change and attempt to remove barriers.*
- *Challenge the status quo to acknowledge the need for change.*
- *Champion the change and enlist others in its pursuit.*
- *Model the change expected of others.*
- *Monitor the emotional impact of change.*

e) **Team Building** (2 Tim 2:22–24)

1   2   3   4   5

Nurturing instrumental relationships.

People with this competence:

- *Cultivate and maintain extensive informal networks.*
- *Seek out relationships that are mutually beneficial.*
- *Build rapport and keep others in the loop.*
- *Make and maintain personal friendships among work associates.*

f) **Networking** (Acts 15:36–41)

1   2   3   4   5

Working with others toward shared goals.

People with this competence:

- *Balance a focus on task with attention to relationships.*
- *Collaborate, sharing plans, information, and resources.*
- *Promote a friendly, cooperative climate.*
- *Spot and nurture opportunities for collaboration.*

g) **Team Performance** (Matt 10:1–6)

1   2   3   4   5

Creating group synergy in pursuing collective goals.

People with this competence:

- *Model team qualities like respect, helpfulness, and cooperation.*
- *Draw all members into active and enthusiastic participation.*
- *Build team identity, esprit de corps, and commitment.*
- *Protect the group and its reputation; share credit.*

OTHER WORKS BY THIS AUTHOR

The Empowered Church

The Empowered Church highlights the distinction between the roles of ministry and leadership. It defines both and in a practical way provides insight and strategies as to how the 'leadership' role of the pastor can be implemented effectively.

....

Re-engineering the Church

In Re-engineering the Church the thorny questions related to church boards are tackled head on and the tools for use in designing or redesigning church structures are explained. The issue of succession planning is addressed along with how to build effective leadership teams. Sample documents are included that can be used in real situations to implement the recommendations in the book.

....

Reflections Vol. 1 - Lives with Purpose

This book of *Reflections* is the first of a new series based on books of the New Testament. Ian has chosen to start with the writings of Luke (his gospel and the book of Acts). There are 96 *Reflections* which will challenge and inspire you. They are soundly grounded in the Scriptures but have a practical outworking and often conclude with a challenge question.

Reflections Vol. 2 – Walking with Christ

Is based on Paul's epistles to the Galatians, Ephesians, Philippians, Colossians and Philemon. It confronts us with the wisdom given to Paul by God which he passed on to the leaders and members of churches he and his team members started.

The Truth for Life Booklet Series

- Generosity
- Prayer and the Ministry of Healing
- Water Baptism
- The Blessing of Communion
- Baptism of the Holy Spirit

THE **JAGELMAN INSTITUTE**
SEEING YOUR WORLD THROUGH LEADERSHIP EYES

www.jaginst.org

Lightning Source UK Ltd.
Milton Keynes UK
UKOW04f0923010716

277405UK00001B/121/P

9 781921 144011